'Matt is a world-class strategist with a wonderful ability to explain how organisations can build and leverage the power of branding to thrive in competitive markets. He is a truly consummate storyteller, and in Four Pillars, he has a great story to tell. Regardless of whether you are new to branding or a seasoned marketer, you should read this book.'

Don O'Sullivan PhD, Professor of Marketing, Melbourne Business School

'Matt gets brands, understands the challenges businesses face and seems to get a genuine kick out of seeing others succeed.'

Ellie Vince, CMO, Brown Family Wine Group

'Meeting Matt is like marketing therapy. I walk out feeling more supercharged than ever.'

Ashik Ahmed, co-founder, Deputy

'Matt gets 'it' before most people even know there is an 'it' to get.'

Alexandra Burt, proprietor, Voyager Estate

'Outrageously articulate, splendidly creative and profoundly pragmatic.'

Colin Pidd, founding partner, ByMany

'A masterful, authentic storyteller.'

Victoria Angove, managing director, Angove Family Winemakers

'With his characteristic wit and incisive wisdom, Matt has distilled what it takes to create a brand that is truly remarkable. If you're looking for clear advice and practical insight on how to scale a business or idea, look no further than *Lessons from Gin*.'

Michael McQueen, international bestselling author and change strategist

T0246736

LESSONS FROM GIN

Business the Four Pillars Way

• • • •

LESSONS FROM GIN

Business the Four Pillars Way

Matt Jones
Co-founder, Four Pillars Gin

WILEY

ISBN: 978-1-394-26837-5

 A catalogue record for this book is available from the National Library of Australia

Registered Office
John Wiley & Sons Australia, Ltd. Level 4, 600 Bourke Street, Melbourne, VIC 3000, Australia

For details of our global editorial offices, customer services, and more information about Wiley products visit us at www.wiley.com.

Wiley also publishes its books in a variety of electronic formats and by print-on-demand. Some content that appears in standard print versions of this book may not be available in other formats.

Cover images: © h.yegho/Shutterstock, © 19 STUDIO/Shutterstock, © Victoria Sergeeva/Shutterstock, © janniwet/Shutterstock
Cover design by Alex Ross Creative
Inside cover photo: © Benito Martin (Sam I Am)
Part I-III opener photos: © Anson Smart
Part IV opener photo: © Mike Emmet
Internal cocktail illustrations: © Octyabr/Adobe Stock
Business icons: © iiierlok_xolms/Adobe Stock
LEGO brick illustration: © sebastian / Adobe Stock

Set in Clarendon URW 9/12pt by Straive, Chennai, India
SKY6BD97A2F-0348-4F36-A925-1864B6382826_102324

For Rebecca, who made all this possible. And for Harper and Jack, who shared a large part of their childhoods with their parents' determination to build something that mattered.

For John, the mentor I'm lucky enough to call my father. And for Eileen, who taught me to value every word (even if I still use too many).

For Cam, Leah, Sally and Stu. The greatest quartet of partners Bec and I could have dreamt of.

For everyone who has ever worked a day or a decade at Four Pillars, and everyone who has ever sold or bought a bottle of the good stuff. Without you, none of these lessons would have been learned.

CONTENTS

ABOUT THE AUTHOR

Matt Jones has enjoyed an eclectic career woven together by the common themes of creative strategy, storytelling, design, experiences and human behaviour.

Matt describes himself as a serial failure and an accidental entrepreneur, having moved from being a government economist to a political strategist to a global brand experience leader before going on to be co-founder of Australia's most loved and successful gin business, Four Pillars Gin.

An economics graduate, Matt's early professional roles took him first to the Defence Intelligence Staff and then HM Treasury in London's Whitehall. After studying for a Master's in International Relations, Matt moved into politics, becoming the head of Economic Section in the legendary Conservative Research Department in 2002, aged just 26. Matt went on to become the Conservative Party's chief political adviser.

In 2006, Matt moved from London to Sydney and from politics to brand strategy, joining the world's largest brand experience firm, Jack Morton Worldwide. Starting out as head of strategy in Australia, Matt moved to take on strategy for Jack Morton New York in 2009 before becoming leader of the Jack Morton global strategy and creative community in 2010.

In 2012, Matt and his young family relocated back to Australia where he set up his own brand purpose consultancy, Better Happy. He handed one of his first business cards to Stuart Gregor at a lunch in

Surry Hills, and within a year Matt, Stu and Stu's best mate Cam were making plans to make gin together.

Today, Matt is the proud co-founder and brand director of Four Pillars Gin, a gin business that has been named the world's best gin producer an extraordinary three times by the International Wine and Spirits Competition in London. Matt is also a passionate keynote speaker, mentor, adviser, board member and collaborator with creative agencies, start-up businesses, corporate brands and not-for-profit organisations. He's also half of Think Story Experience, a boutique advisory firm he runs with his partner Rebecca Bourne Jones.

Matt describes himself the same way he did on his first Jack Morton business card back in 2006, as a creative strategist. You can learn more about Matt's work, experience, passions and interests on his website www.thinkstoryexperience.com.

PROLOGUE

What this book is.
And what it's not.

Welcome, friends. Before we begin, let's make sure you're in the right place. Because this is not the definitive story of Four Pillars Gin. At best, only a third of that story is mine to tell. So here it is, my side of the gin-soaked story and the lessons I took from over a decade of helping to build a world-class gin business.

Back in 2012, I crossed paths with two of the most extraordinary and talented humans I will ever meet: Cam and Stu. These two men would go on to change gin in Australia and change my life in the process: Cam with his drive, pragmatism and ability to become one of the world's great gin distillers; Stu with his entrepreneurial creative instincts, optimism and unparalleled ability to open doors and build relationships. Without them at the heart of everything, Four Pillars simply wouldn't have happened.

This book is the story of the things I did, or at least the things I contributed to—the value I (hopefully) added. The ways I helped shape how the Four Pillars story unfolded and how we successfully built an extraordinary business together and, in the process, led a craft spirits revolution in Australia that saw the number of distilleries in this country grow from under 30 to over 600 in a decade.

At the heart of my side of the Four Pillars story is how we ensured that the world-class gin product at the heart of our business always (or at least more often than not) got the credit it deserved and benefited from the positive bias that would help it grow. Bias is a concept I'm going to talk about a lot.

I will share some stories about how we made the world's best gin at Four Pillars and how we made sure the world knew about it. And, when all the talk of gin gets too much to take without reaching for a bottle of Four Pillars, there are also a few drinks breaks and recipes along the way too.

The book is divided into four key parts, reflecting what I see as the four key parts to building a business like Four Pillars Gin. They aren't perfectly chronological, although I do start at the beginning and end at the end (it's the middle where timelines get a little mixed up). Instead of being chronologically accurate, I've tried to bundle the stories and lessons in four big themes: *thinking* clearly about your business; *crafting* the core elements of your business; *sharing* the fruits of your craft with the world and getting the credit you deserve for it; and *growing* in the face of change, disruption, new opportunities but also new challenges.

I'd like to think these four phases are relevant whether you're a small start-up business or an established player. I'd also like to think you can apply this thinking to things that aren't businesses, such as a charity, an organisation, a movement or even the development of your own personal brand and career.

Each of the four sections of this book contains four 'useful bits', where I pull out the gin-soaked lessons from our experience and show how they can be applied to just about anything. They're definitely not rocket science, but they are (hopefully) a helpful guide to thinking in useful ways about the four key stages of starting and/or scaling any business:

1. How to think clearly about the business you're going to build. What decisions are you really making? Are you clear on the implications and reasoning behind those decisions?

2. How to identify and commit to the core craft at the heart of your business. What's your why? What's your how? And what business are you really in?

3. How to share the fruits of your craft and ensure you receive the credit you deserve for the value you create. And how to think about the role of emotion, design, storytelling and experiences in growing your business.

4. And, finally, how to navigate growth and change as your business succeeds, as it evolves and faces new challenges and opportunities. How to know when to stay the course and when to adjust to your new realities.

In other words, these sections are no replacement for a fully formed business, product, brand or marketing strategy—over time, you'll need all of those things—but they will help you think at a high level. And sometimes that high-level clarity is all you need to keep moving forward with confidence and conviction.

For anyone reading this book who loves gin, I hope it offers some fresh perspectives on what has made Four Pillars (I believe) the most exciting, innovative, uncompromising and simply delicious gin producer on the planet. And for anyone with their own idea for a business, a product, an organisation, a movement—whatever it may be—I hope this book gives you some frameworks to build your own layers of brand bias around your efforts, and ensure that you and whatever value you create get the credit you so richly deserve.

Lastly, please don't think I'm right—about anything really—whether it's how to build a great brand or how to stir the perfect martini. As the saying goes, 'all models are wrong, but some are useful'. I hope some of the models I talk about in this book are useful. And, perhaps by showing where these thought processes took the Four Pillars business, they can help you think about how to navigate wherever you want to go.

So don't read this book if you're looking for scientific marketing facts. There are no sure things when it comes to starting and growing a business. There are just decisions and choices to make. I hope this book prompts you to think about and make enough of the right decisions and choices. And I hope it inspires you to have fun and keep smiling while you do it.

Few of us can do what Cameron did (whether it's when he ran around a 400-metre track fast enough to get to the Olympics in 1996 or when he became the most awarded gin distiller on the planet), and I can say with confidence that I'll never meet another person with the room-filling charisma and personality of Stuart. But we've all got something we do well, something that gives us energy, and something we want to do with all that talent and passion. I hope this book inspires you to think about how to make the most of those possibilities.

And now, with all that said, and with those caveats in place, it's time to begin. Let's start a gin business.

PART ONE

Thinking

PART ONE

Thinking

ONE

In the beginning, there was a decision

Sometimes, very rarely, you come across a genuinely big idea. An idea that stops you in your tracks. An idea to make or do something wildly groundbreaking and completely novel. Perhaps even an idea that can change the world. This is not a book about big ideas like that.

In truth, there are few big, transformative ideas to be found. Most ideas (even the ones that do go on to change the world) are variations on previously explored themes—take Uber, which started out as an idea for a limo service that showed where your car was on a map (which, itself, was inspired by a device Daniel Craig's James Bond used in the film *Casino Royale*). Or take the 'idea' to make gin. It's hardly new. To make gin is simply to follow in the footsteps of Dutch genever makers from the 1600s and British gin barons from the 1700s (more on the history of gin in Chapter 3).

So, this is not a book about big ideas; instead, it's about small ideas. The small ideas that, together, can help grow a business (and a brand... we'll touch on that distinction later too). The small ideas that result from countless daily acts and decisions. So, really, this is a book about decisions.

As you get older, you realise there are so many truths no one tells you when you're younger—like how much of parenting is actually logistics. Or, in this case, how much of the founding and leading of a business is just the seemingly endless task of making decisions (and living with the decisions you make). No wonder I felt so exhausted after the three COVID-affected years of 2020, 2021 and 2022. We had made so many rapid decisions on the fly and against a background of such uncertainty and constant change. It wasn't the school at home that exhausted me...it was the decision making at work.

Starting a business is merely a decision, one decision that leads to many others. Each of those decisions amounts to a small idea. Even the decision to not do something is, itself, a small idea with consequences and impact. Get enough of these small ideas right, execute enough of them brilliantly and you might be onto something. This is the truth of most businesses. There are no shortcuts. No magic bullets. No game-changing big ideas. Just decisions, choices, priorities, compromises, mistakes, hustle and execution. But I'm already jumping ahead because we haven't got to the first decision yet.

The decision to make gin wasn't mine. It was Stu's and Cam's.

Cam is an Olympian. Both literally and figuratively. Literally, because he dragged his body around a running track fast enough to make Australia's 400-metre relay team at Atlanta in 1996 (he made the semis, if you're wondering, and in some very questionable running shorts). Figuratively, because he has a capacity for determination, execution and excellence that puts him in the top-three people I would take into any battle with me. He also happens to be wildly creative, have an extraordinary palate and is one of the funniest, most engaging people I've ever spent time with. Yep, in short, if you were designing the perfect co-founder and distiller for a craft gin business, you'd end up with Cameron Mackenzie.

And then there's Stuart. If generosity was an Olympic discipline, Stu would doubtless be an Olympian too. Like Cam, he's genuinely hilarious. Like Cam, he has an extraordinary palate. And, like Cam, he had spent decades in the Australian booze industry. Unlike Cam, Stu had gone on to build one of Australia's great communications agencies, specialising in the food and drink space. So Stu knew people, he knew business and he knew stuff. Between the two of them, we had the raw material to do something special in gin.

In the past, Stu and Cam had decided to make wine together (twice), buy stakes in racehorses together (too often) and not work in the same office together (again). And now here they were making a new decision. To make gin together. But this decision was different. It came with a caveat. This time, they would get a third partner involved: me.

Cam and Stu had both worked in and around the wine industry for years, both with a deep knowledge and passion for wine and spirits of all types. Cameron had spent time getting his hands dirty in production, operations and distribution roles, while Stu had built an extraordinary PR and communications business, Liquid Ideas, and had become arguably one of Australia's most sought-after strategic partners for wine brands (and all kinds of food, drink and hospitality businesses). These two, in other words, were made to make gin together.

If Cam and Stu were both made to go into the gin business, I was the less obvious contributor to the success of Four Pillars. My background is an eclectic one, starting off as a UK Government economist, moving first into politics as a policy adviser then a speechwriter then a communication strategist, moving into the world of brand and brand agencies.

By the time I met Cam and Stu, I had spent 15 years advising people and businesses, from future prime ministers like Theresa May and David Cameron to global brands like Samsung and Google. Locally, I had advised future unicorns (i.e. billion-dollar companies) like Deputy, and all manner of great Australian businesses and brands from AMP and the NRMA to Voyager Estate and St. Agnes.

But giving advice is one thing; putting your own advice into practice is quite another. So, while I didn't lack confidence in my abilities, I hadn't yet had the opportunity to use my skills and experience to create something myself. And now I was going to do it in a category where I had near zero professional experience (albeit a fair bit of experience as a consumer).

What drew me to gin? In short, it seemed to me that gin provided that rarest of opportunities: to create a truly differentiated (and better) product that would still need creative thinking and brand-building to get it the credit it deserved. As someone who has never been a fan of traditional, advertising-led marketing and who believes the world is already full of enough stuff and doesn't need more commoditised clutter, the opportunity to help create better gin and to make sure Cam's and Stu's efforts would get the credit they deserved was too tempting to say 'no' to. I was in.

In moving from that first decision (to make gin, not tonic) to that next decision (to find a third partner) to the next decisions (the partner would be me and I would say 'yes' to the opportunity), we were learning our first important lessons about starting a business.

There's no one thing that defines a business and determines whether it will succeed, fail or (in many cases) tick along doing neither. A business is simply the sum total of the consequences of its decisions.

Stu, Cam and I have made literally thousands of decisions over a decade of building Four Pillars Gin. I guess we must have got enough of them right that I'm sitting here writing this book. And, in the next chapter, I'll explore some of the ways that we (sometimes consciously, sometimes unconsciously, and sometimes with pure serendipity) approached making our first big decisions together.

TWO

Okay, so we're doing this. But doing what, exactly?

I've told the Four Pillars story ~~hundreds~~ thousands of times over the past decade, and someone will always ask, 'Where did the idea of making gin come from?' And I've always been keen to own the fact that making gin was not an idea, it was a decision.

I'm not trying to be contrary here or split linguistic hairs for the sake of it. I'm trying to help clarify what I suspect is, for most of us, the experience of creating a business, which is to say that we make a decision to take action and do something.

Writing this now can risk being a reinvention of history, a making sense of what happened in a way that feels far more structured and strategic than it really was. So, now, here's the truth of how we moved through these steps.

It was 2012, and I'd been working with Stu and his Liquid Ideas team for a few months. It was clear we shared a perspective on how brands got built and what worked in this new socially wired landscape. While our working and communications styles are quite different, our ways of thinking are remarkably aligned, and from day one I felt this was someone I could work with and learn from. In addition, we both loved food and wine (about which he knew infinitely more than me) and shared a passion for Manchester United. The building blocks of friendship and partnership were in place.

Stu wanted me to meet his mate Cameron. He and Cam had played around with making wine together for years, first under the Donny Goodmac brand, then as part of Dirty Three Wines (where Marcus and Lisa are still making sensational wine to this day down in Gippsland, Victoria). Now, they were talking about making gin, but hadn't got serious about it.

Our first dinner in Surry Hills was a chance for Cam to meet me. I don't know what Stu had told him in advance, but Cam was a natural sceptic when it came to bullshit-peddling, self-styled, brand-marketing gurus, so it was probably an opportunity for him to judge whether he could work with me or not. The smart money was on not.

Somehow I passed the test, and the second dinner happened at Cam's place in Healesville in the Yarra Valley. We talked about gin, and gin drinks, and Stu even invented a signature serve for the gin we hadn't yet made. He called it the Keating (gin, tonic, Campari, lime — sophisticated, perhaps even a bit pretentious, slightly bitter, just like our former PM). The next day, pretty worse for wear, we talked more over breakfast and I walked away with the job of writing up our first (very basic) business and brand plan.

Two dinners, one hungover breakfast and one PowerPoint presentation, and suddenly this thing felt real, and we were agreeing to put some money in the bank to send Stu and Cam to the USA to learn more. Perhaps, ironically for a business that has been shaped so much by the fact that all three co-founders were bald/forty-something/ experienced, we had the humility to begin by identifying what we didn't know. In short, we didn't know anything about making gin.

At this stage, some context would be helpful. In 2012, there were fewer than 30 distilleries operating in Australia, and Tasmanian whisky was arguably the only Australian spirit making waves (with the exception of Bundy, of course). As I write this in 2024, there are over 600 distilleries operating in Australia. And between them they make around 300 different gins. It's hard to imagine how little precedent there was in Australia for what we were about to do.

So Cam and Stu went to the USA to see what a real craft distilling scene looked like.

It may also have been true that Stu and Cam fancied a road trip, but either way, off they went to drive down the West Coast from Seattle to LA, stopping at over 30 craft distilleries along the way. They were going to be the drivers of the product (I knew, and still know, my place in the business!), and what happened on that trip is their story to tell. For me, three critical things came out of their travels.

First, Cam was essential to the whole enterprise, and lucky for us, he was hooked. He was going to be our master distiller, and he was going to invest the time and effort to teach himself to make world-class gin. Without his commitment over that early period, the Four Pillars dream simply wouldn't have happened, and there would have been nothing for me and Stu to help grow. It was Cam's drive and natural talent (supported always by Stu's incredible palate) that created the conditions for us to execute our plan and gave us the right to succeed. I am under no illusions that, without this secret ingredient, Four Pillars would have been nothing.

Second, a great distiller would need a great still, and every time Stu and Cam had been blown away by the quality of a spirit on their travels, they would find a CARL still was responsible. Based on the outskirts of Stuttgart in Germany, the Carl family have been hand-making copper stills the same way for over a century. We had to have one—no matter how long the waiting list or how expensive they were. We paid our deposit and got our names down for a 450-litre gin still with all the bells and whistles (all up, we were going to need over half-a-million bucks just to make a single bottle...at least to the standards we were aspiring to). This was getting very real. But we were still ten months away from getting our hands on our shiny new gin machine.

Cam entered what we fondly remember as his *Breaking Bad* phase, purchasing a small laboratory still, and (Cam claims) having to persuade the local cops that he was cooking up lemon myrtle not crystal meth. What he was doing, of course, related to the third major aim of that US road trip: figuring out how to make a truly modern Australian gin.

What Cam and Stu experienced in the US was a craft distilling scene that was hell-bent on originality and local expression. The Americans, unsurprisingly, weren't trying to replicate London Dry Gin, but were instead forging their own paths. Cam and Stu were inspired by great gins from producers like Junipero, Ransom and St George's, and came back feeling liberated that we, too, could skip the ubiquitous London Dry-style gin and go straight to something more distinctive and unique. But that, in turn, required us to make new decisions, starting with: if we weren't going to make gin in a recognised traditional style, what the hell were we going to make?

THREE

Riding the fourth gin wave

I've already noted that the distilling landscape in Australia was still in its infancy, but this is probably the right time to quickly recap the state of the gin category in 2012 more broadly. As I saw it (thanks to the rapid education I received from Stu and Cam), there had been four waves of gin, each with different levels of maturity, and only three of them had come to Australia at any meaningful scale.

The first was classic London Dry Gin, aka nana's favourite tipple—think Gordons gin. This is the gin that gave me such a horrifyingly bad hangover back in 1998 that it put me off gin for another four years (in hindsight, it was my fault, not the gin's).

On a good day, great London Dry Gin smells like a pine forest; on a bad day, it smells and, arguably, tastes like Pine O Cleen. London Dry Gin is traditionally made to precise and narrow specifications and, typically, with just a handful of botanicals, led and dominated by juniper. It's as old as the hills, with benchmarks including Gordon's (launched in 1769), Tanqueray (1830) and Beefeater (1863).

The late twentieth century saw a second, new wave of gin led by Bombay Sapphire (launched in 1987) and Tanqueray No. Ten (launched in 2000). These gins were still technically London Dry, but lighter in style, more botanically focused and often used vapour infusion to achieve a more delicate flavour profile. With gins like Bombay on the scene in the 1990s, gin was starting to get its mojo back, but it needed one more push from a new brand with a very novel approach.

Hendrick's was launched in 1999, and represented the third style of gin: contemporary. Using two stills, two signature botanicals (cucumber and rose) and one signature serve (a G&T with cucumber), Hendrick's quickly became a dominant player in the new category of super-premium contemporary gin.

By 2013, Hendrick's was dominant in Australia, commanding over 60 per cent of the super-premium gin category (gin sold at over $70 a bottle). Fortunately for us, Hendrick's domination of the category was helping to liberate drinkers' ideas of what gin could be. And this was further augmented by the arrival of a key non-gin player on the scene: Fever-Tree. I'll talk a bit more about what makes Fever-Tree (and good tonic in general) so special in the G&T drinks break on page 90.

Fever-Tree was part of a drinks revolution that was setting the scene for the fourth gin wave, elevating the gin and tonic with a focus on using quality tonic. Meanwhile, the rise of hugely influential bartenders, like Dale DeGroff, Sasha Petraske and Dick Bradsell, was helping to bring back the popularity of classic (often gin-led) cocktails.

Now that twentieth-century trends of vodka, flair bartending and tragically bad G&Ts were all behind us, a new century was bringing a gin boom, a resurgence of classic cocktails made with a few exceptional ingredients. The G&T was once again seen as a drink of choice for people under the age of 80, all of which set the stage for what was coming.

The fourth gin wave (which is still rolling on as I type) brought with it a new world of locally made (but globally famous) craft gin, with Sipsmith in London as its champion. This was the movement that had not yet come to Australia, and, to be fair, no one was clamouring for it.

While there were some inspiring early movers in this space, most notably a gin called The West Winds Distillers from WA, I don't think anyone was losing sleep over the lack of a great Aussie craft gin.

In short, there was an opportunity here. And, if we played our cards right, we had the chance to be at the front of this fourth craft gin wave in Australia. But, we also needed to be realistic that we were about to start solving a problem that no one was asking to be solved.

Maybe that wasn't a bad thing. As the strategist Alex Smith has noted, sometimes listening to customers is the last thing you should do, as customers can only tell you what they want based on what they know (leading, as Alex puts it, to commodification of your offer and distraction from your original strategy).

So what did we decide to make? In short, we decided to make a modern Australian gin. After all, why would you set up a gin distillery 16 000 kilometres from London and make your first move a London Dry–style gin? Again, to paraphrase Alex Smith, we did something all businesses should do (but many fear), which was to be bad at something. In our case we chose to be bad at making classic London Dry Gin.

To be fair, Cameron could have made a great London Dry Gin. The point was that he didn't even try. Because, just as we had made the decision to be uniquely focused on gin, we wanted to tighten that even further and be utterly focused on making modern Australian gin—gin we could only make because of the unique opportunities afforded to us by making gin in Australia. It was that extremely narrow definition of our focus, our craft, that ultimately spawned the extraordinary creativity that has defined Four Pillars.

Don't listen to your customers (if we had, they would have told us that they didn't need an Australian alternative to Hendrick's), choose to be bad at things (in our case, making any other spirit than gin), and place your creativity within narrow constraints (we were modern Australian gin-makers working to self-imposed and highly exacting standards). These were all counterintuitive decisions we made in those early days that played a critical role in setting the long-term direction for Four Pillars. Let's just take that last one as an example:

the constraint to only make gin and only make that gin in a modern Australian style.

There's nothing lazier than creativity without constraint. It allows all manner of off-strategy ideas (that the business has neither the right nor the ability to execute well) to distract from the core. Instead, true creative thinking comes from embracing constraints. Constraints that may, at first, seem confining, frustrating even, but which ultimately push you to places that would otherwise have never been found and explored, like combining gin with Shiraz grapes. But again, that's all in the future.

A quick recap

So we had just made our next big decisions:

- We were going to work as a trio to make gin together.

- We were only going to make gin.

- We were going to make gin in a uniquely modern Australian style.

- Cameron was going to be our master distiller and would focus on acquiring the learning and experience required to make world-class gin.

- We were going to invest in the best gin still we could find, made by CARL in Germany.

- Establishing modern Australian craft gin would take time (so we were going to need enough cash to stay in the game long enough to succeed).

- We were going to need some substantial start-up capital.

DRINKS BREAK NO.1:

The (Gin) Martini

I never liked gin. In fact, my first and most abiding memory of drinking gin was throwing my guts up in the bathroom of an ex-girlfriend's house in London in 1998. Gordon's and tonic out of a pint glass was the culprit. The smell, that cloying Pine O Cleen odour, was something I felt lingering in my nostrils for weeks afterwards. And the dislike of gin stayed with me for years.

Gin's first chance for redemption came four years later in 2002, when one of New York's most iconic bars, Milk & Honey, opened in London's Soho. It was a member's bar, and I signed up immediately—not because I had the palate to appreciate the quality of the drinks being made there, but because I wanted to be part of something cool.

Little did I know that what was happening at London venues like Milk & Honey was setting the scene for an extraordinary resurgence in gin. And that, 11 years later in 2013, I would be launching a gin brand in Australia that would be the direct beneficiary of the momentum that was building back in the early 2000s in that very bar in London.

I had no idea any of that was happening. All I knew was that Milk & Honey was cool and I wasn't (but wanted to be). I knew that being a member of a Soho bar with an unmarked door on Poland Street, being ushered past a velvet curtain, being in the room and in the know felt good (and, I hoped, made me look good). And I knew that these drinks tasted good, and nothing like the Long Island iced teas of my university years.

One of the drinks that saw its reputation revived in the 2000s was the classic gin Martini (stirred, never shaken). I'd had a few vodka Martinis in my time, but the idea of gin in a Martini scared me thanks to my 1998 trauma. Fast-forward to today and I can't imagine a Martini made with anything other than gin.

At Four Pillars, we've always said that the martini is the ultimate test of a gin. It's a simple drink, but super expressive and allows almost infinite opportunities for subtle personalisation. One of the things I learned from Stu, Cam and the amazing bartenders I've spent time with at Four Pillars is that the Martini (like so many great drinks) has four key ingredients. So, yes, the gin and the vermouth are critical, but so is the ice (giving the drink both coldness and dilution) and the garnish.

Here are a few of my favourite Martini serves (and no, you don't have to make them with Four Pillars Gin, but it helps).

No.1: Classic Gin Martini

60 ml Rare Dry Gin
15 ml dry vermouth
Orange
Ice

Stir Four Pillars Rare Dry Gin with dry vermouth in a mixing glass with lots of ice. Strain it into a cocktail glass and garnish with a twist of orange peel.

Stirred not shaken?

James Bond got this one wrong. Shaking causes the ice to break into shards, diluting your Martini more than is ideal. By stirring, we keep the ice intact, maximising the chilling of the drink without causing too much dilution.

Which vermouth to use?

Stu would tell you that the best white vermouths come from France, so start by trying Dolin or Noilly Prat.

No.2: Perfect Gin Martini

60 ml Olive Leaf Gin
15 ml dry vermouth
Olives
Extra virgin olive oil
Ice

We made our Olive Leaf Gin to be naturally savoury and textural, making it (we think) the ultimate Martini gin. Stir Olive Leaf Gin with dry vermouth in a mixing glass with lots of ice. Garnish with an olive or three on a cocktail pick and a few drops of extra virgin olive oil.

Dirty Martini

Feel free to disagree, but we don't think adding olive brine makes it a better drink. Fresh olives, olive oil and our Olive Leaf Gin should be just perfect.

No.3: The 50:50 Martini

Your favourite gin
Dry vermouth
Twist or olive
Ice

Stir equal parts of your favourite gin and dry vermouth in a mixing glass with ice, then garnish with whatever takes your fancy (twist or olive). The key here is the longer, 'wetter' drink thanks to the generous pour of vermouth.

How much is too much?

Winston Churchill is said to have simply waved his glass towards France and said that was enough vermouth in his Martini, but some might simply call that a glass of cold gin. Vermouth at its best is delicious and aromatic (just keep your vermouth in the fridge and consume it within a month). Made properly with fresh, lively vermouth, this is my favourite Martini serve.

No.4: The Martinez

45 ml of any barrel-aged gin
20 ml sweet red vermouth
5 ml of Bénédictine liqueur
Bitters
Orange
Ice

Start with 45 ml of any barrel-aged gin (at Four Pillars, we love making this drink with Australian Christmas Gin) and 20 ml of sweet red vermouth (this time, maybe go Italian and start with Cocchi from Torino). Add in Bénédictine liqueur and a couple of dashes of bitters, stir over ice, strain and serve with an orange twist.

The neglected classic

The Martinez was actually the precursor to the simpler and more refined martini, and deserves far more recognition than it gets. For me, it's a natural bridge from the Martinez into the world of the Negroni, arguably the world's greatest cocktail. We'll get to the Negroni in drinks break number three on page 142.

FOUR

Starting as you mean to go on — every decision matters most

Isuspect the majority of people reading this book aren't starting something. You're already doing something (maybe running a business or simply trying to be the most effective version of yourself in whatever way is important to you). So your questions, your challenges, are: How to grow that something? Where to focus? What to do? And what not to do, or at least do less of?

But for those of you who are still in the starting phase, it's worth reflecting on what a special/precious/fragile/scary time that starting phase is (even when you don't realise it at the time).

As I noted in Chapter 3 (before we went for a drinks break), business is just decision making, and those decisions seem to come at you thick and fast in the early days. There's a temptation to just get on with it, to prioritise action, to believe that all momentum is good momentum, but to think in that way is to fail to see both the preciousness and the fragility of these early (or even pre-launch) days.

In hindsight, there are many sliding doors moments that could have taken your business, your idea, down a very different path. In our case, although we appeared to have locked in most of the big decisions after Stu and Cam returned from the USA, the reality is that those decisions were just the tip of the decision-making iceberg.

The next big decision we made (and could, frankly, have ignored until it became an issue) was how we were going to work together. One of the most exciting things about the Four Pillars business (apart from the gin, which is really the only thing that matters) is that, from day one, I have had the privilege of partnering with two people who are completely at the top of their game—and now we had to choose who was going to captain this gin-powered ship.

Stu was the natural leader of the group, as he is in any room he enters. He definitely has big leader energy and is quite possibly the most charismatic and connected human in Australian business. He's also an extraordinarily intelligent, incisive thinker with a rare combination of commercial acumen, communications expertise and genuine creativity.

Cam was also an obvious choice, as he was the one who was going to be building the distillery and making the gin while Stu and I contributed from the sidelines (at least until the business was making enough money to be able to pay for some of our time too).

But to elevate either of them to be the sole managing director or CEO of our start-up would have missed the power of the trio. It would have made it that much harder to get the best out of our trio of superpowers (or, at least, our diverse skills and mindsets).

We sat down early on and agreed we would be co-CEOs. This raised two challenging questions. The first was, will anyone take us seriously if we put a three co-CEO model into our investor memorandum (we'll talk more about fundraising in Chapter 5)? That was an easy concern to dismiss considering that the Lowy family had successfully grown the Westfield empire under the same model. The second, more material, question was, if we are all co-CEOs, how will we decide what to do in the event of disagreement? How we answered this question is, I believe, key to the success we've had with Four Pillars.

My view was clear: we had made the decision to make gin unanimously, and every decision we had made so far had been made unanimously. So, why shouldn't we continue in the same way?

To require unanimity on all major decisions moving forward would do two things. First, it would require us all to be more rigorous in our thinking. Only having to pick off and persuade one of your two partners of the rightness of your approach, catching them in a weak moment or talking to their personal biases, would allow much more faulty thinking to prevail. Requiring every major decision to be supported by both your partners required a much higher standard of thinking. Second, it would require us all to be reasonable grown-ups capable of compromise, understanding when to dig in on a major point of strategy, and when to bow to the expertise or leadership of your partners on a point of nuance or subjectivity.

With the co-CEO model locked in (and enshrined in our shareholders' agreement), the next thing was to agree how we would work together. If I'm honest, I don't remember how much we talked about it explicitly, but it became very clear very fast what areas each of us would take the lead in. I want to explore that in detail here as I think (possibly by luck more than judgement), we landed on a perfect balance of overlapping empathy and distinctive specialism in how we divided and conquered.

First, the overlaps: Stu and Cam both have exceptional palates, but, ultimately, it was Cameron who threw himself into learning how to become a world-class gin distiller with the same level of focus, commitment and bloody-minded determination that had got him to the Olympics. So it was Cam who would make the final calls on flavour.

Meanwhile, Stu and I were both working in the marketing space: me coming at things from a brand strategy and brand experience point of view; Stu from the point of view of public relations and earned media. with the added bonus of having ten times my experience when it came to actually building and running a business.

So our roles and responsibilities were becoming crystal clear. Cam would make gin and make things happen—and make sure we didn't blow ourselves up while we did it. Stu would make friends and make noise in the media, in the drinks industry, with our customers and with our partners. And I would make sense and make things look good.

So, my tasks included shaping and codifying our strategies as a business and as a brand; articulating the logic of what we were trying to do in everything from investor presentations to brand plans to crowdfunding campaigns to board meetings and long-term visions; and developing the aesthetics and materiality of the wider brand world we would build around the gin.

All three of us contributed to all aspects of the business, but the understanding was there from very early on that we each had areas of absolute expertise and we would take ownership and lead in those areas. The areas of overlap between our experience and expertise also helped us make better decisions.

A perfect example of this was how I took responsibility for the overall strategy of the brand, both articulating it and keeping us on track, while Stu took the lead on the critical role that relationships would play in growing our brand (both with the media and with the trade). The result was that our brand strategy was taken seriously, and our brand tone of voice always had a levity, a warmth and a smile.

For ten years, the three of us acted as co-CEOs of Four Pillars Gin, each ultimately responsible for the growth and strength of the whole business, but each with a unique set of accountabilities that relate to our personal passion and expertise. What made it work so well was that we all understood and committed to what we were personally responsible for, but we also all had a deep respect for each other's areas of effort and expertise. This model remained broadly unchanged for a whole decade.

USEFUL BIT #1:
DECISION CHECKLIST

Welcome to the first Useful Bit. These are the parts of the book designed to help you apply some of the things Stu, Cam and I learned over a decade of growing Four Pillars to your own world, whatever it is you're looking to build or grow. To think of these Useful Bits in another way, they encapsulate the kinds of questions I'd ask you and thoughts I'd offer you if we were together talking about your growth ambitions.

This first Useful Bit is anchored by a simple checklist. It's the most basic of business-planning models, inviting you to question and think clearly about the decision (or decisions) you're about to make. But before we ask the right questions, I want to begin with a classic (but usually wrong) question.

What's your big idea?

The idea of the 'big idea' appeals. It implies that some genius silver bullet, some blinding insight, some radical innovation can make the difference for your business. But, as we discussed in Chapter 1, success will likely be dependent on a vast array of factors, none of which rely on a big idea, but which are instead the result of countless small, everyday decisions that cumulatively shape the business you build.

Ideas such as to make gin. To open a restaurant. To set up a business. To write a book. These are all decisions. In the case of making gin, by definition, there's no original big idea here—the idea to turn juniper berries into a distilled spirit is hundreds of years old.

Many of you reading this book may also have similarly 'big idea–free' plans. That's okay. A small idea (or multiple small ideas) can be your anchor. A plan can simply be to create a better something; a different something; a something delivered or served in a better way; a something targeted forensically at a narrowly defined, passionate, under-served audience.

And doing things better, or differently, is less about having the silver bullet of a big idea and much more about making consistently good decisions to deliver consistently excellent small ideas.

In other words, building something is less about having a big idea and more about having the clarity to make the right decisions consistently, time and time again.

So how to think about this? Let's start with the first of those decisions, the decision to begin. The decision to build something, to start something, to launch something. Something you believe will create value in the world—even if there's no 'big idea' at the heart of it.

Here are five simple lenses you can use to interrogate and strengthen your plans, sharpening your thinking, clarifying what decision or decisions you're really making, building conviction, and (sometimes) helping you conclude that this would be the wrong course of action. I've called it a decision checklist, but I'm not sure that's the best name as it's not an exercise of putting ticks in boxes. These thought processes are never done (as facts and events keep changing). But making sure you've thought about each of these five lenses should put you in a better place to move forward:

Information. Opportunity. Decision. Execution. Edge.

You can apply these lenses to both big decisions (should I start my own distillery?), medium-sized decisions (should we create a new product?) or even small decisions (should we send that customer email?). The thought process around making the decision is roughly the same.

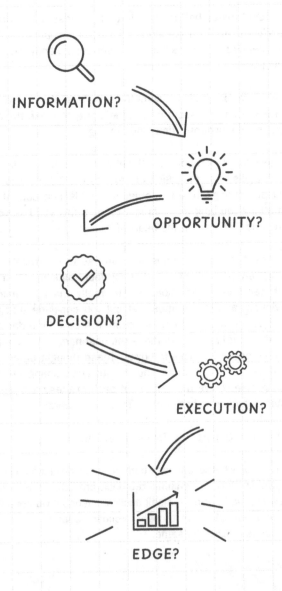

INFORMATION?

OPPORTUNITY?

DECISION?

EXECUTION?

EDGE?

Here's how you might work through those lenses.

Information

Do I have enough *information* about the decision I'm making, about the category I'm entering and about the consumer I'm serving? Do I know enough? Have I researched enough? Who could I speak to to give me deeper, more accurate insight into this decision?

Opportunity

Does my take on this (potentially unoriginal) idea have a sense of purpose, a real problem to solve and a viable audience willing to pay for that solution? Is there, in short, an *opportunity* to create value for someone (value that they would be willing to pay for)?

Decision

What *decision* am I really making here? What business am I getting myself into? What will I need to be good at to deliver on the opportunity? Am I clear on the requirements (and risks) of the decision I'm making?

Execution

Do I have the ability, the means, the knowledge, the subject matter expertise, the relationships, the partners, the resources, the personal capability to *execute* on this decision? If not, how can I build that capability?

Edge

Assuming others will make a similar decision, what gives me the right to be successful? How differentiated is my ability to execute on this big decision? Why, of all the people who could do this, am I the one to make this happen and to succeed? What's my *edge* and am I focused on making the most of it? Will this decision talk to (and amplify) my natural advantages?

How does your big idea feel now? Are you clearer on the decision you're making? Do you feel, with conviction, that it's the right decision? Will your decision create value for someone else? And do you now have clarity about what it will take to turn that decision into success?

If you're still feeling good about your answers to these broad questions, maybe it's time to take the next step.

FIVE

It's never too early to think about your why

More decisions were made, more paths defined by the choices we made. To focus on gin. To place quality above everything else. To create the space and time for Cameron to become a world-class gin-maker. To work together as co-CEOs. To make modern Australian (but not stridently Australian) gin. But there were still big decisions left to make.

When you're starting a business, you get asked lots of questions (and you ask yourself lots of questions) along the lines of: Why are you doing this? What's your ambition? What's your exit strategy? What gives you the right to succeed? And the truth is that you need to slow down and disentangle these questions from each other, because it's a lot to think about. And, if you're anything like me, Stu and Cam back in 2013, you also have a day job to do and a family to take care of, so these questions don't get nearly the attention they deserve.

Nonetheless, the delay between ordering Wilma (we'd already named her after Cam's late mum so she could have her name etched on the front) from CARL in Germany and her arriving in Australia gave us the chance to think these questions through. In hindsight, the answers we came to addressed two of the biggest questions (and the many sub-questions) any business or organisation faces.

1. **What is you purpose and craft?**

   Why do you exist? Why do you matter? Why are you valued? And what is it you do that gives you that right to be valued?

2. **What is your mindset and ambition?**

   How do you need to think (and act) every day to keep you on track? Where, ultimately, are you heading? What is success for you?

But, first I want to start with a confession. We were lucky, as almost all successful businesses are. We got lucky with our timing, and plenty of other things went our way too (things also went against us, as we'll talk about later). But our luck is something I'm proud of, because to paraphrase the John Milton line (one of my dad's favourite business quotes), luck was the residue of our design.

There's a truth that many business, brand and marketing gurus don't want you to believe: a great deal of building a successful business is luck. Ignore the marketing theocrats and growth hackers who peddle certainty, and know that building a successful business depends a great deal on intangibles and uncontrollables, including luck. But it's also true that, by thinking clearly about your business, by designing first and acting second, you can make your business luckier.

The idea that 'luck is the residue of design' sums up perfectly why Four Pillars enjoyed more than its fair share of luck over its first ten years—because we took the time to design the future and because we locked several foundational principles into the DNA of Four Pillars before we'd even begun, starting with the biggest question of all: why?

Simon Sinek has popularised the idea of beginning with purpose and having the big 'why' question answered. In this way, he reasons, brands can connect with a sense of higher purpose and create a deeper and more motivating connection with their customers.

For me, starting with 'why' is about also embracing another key ingredient for business success that I think runs counter to much of our modern hype culture: humility. In deciding to make gin in Australia (remember, it was a decision not a big idea), we also had the humility to recognise that we were solving a problem that no one was asking to be solved. So, we needed to get really clear on our 'why'. Why were we doing this? Why should anyone care? And why did we have a right to succeed?

For us, the answers were all found in that core definition of who we wanted to be as a business: modern Australian gin-makers.

We believed (and still do) that gin is the most versatile spirit on earth. Beyond being based on a canvas of juniper, gin offers the maker enormous creative possibility and versatility. And we also believed that Australia, with our unique natural environment, our botanicals, our access to fresh produce and our unparalleled flavour culture, should be the best place on earth to explore the possibilities of gin. But someone needed to do the work. Why not us?

So that became the cornerstone of our purpose, the first and most important strand of our DNA: to elevate the craft of distilling gin in Australia. And, by doing that in Australia, we would end up elevating the craft of gin worldwide. That, surely, was a big ambition that people would get behind.

The logic, to borrow Cameron's way of phrasing it, was pretty simple: nowhere tasted like Australia, so if we simply focused every day on distilling that, then nothing would taste like our Australian gin. That simple thought process got us to the second strand of our purpose around drinks.

We recognised that gin was, for most people, just an ingredient. So, our gin would only be as good as the drinks people made with it. That meant we would need to be a business that celebrated the craft of the cocktail and, in turn, celebrated and empowered the people making drinks, both in bars and at home.

The third strand of our purpose was around modern Australia. The irony was that, back in 2013, Australia's reputation as a home for world-class food and drink was still in its infancy overseas. If you walked the streets of any hip neighbourhood in global cities from Berlin to Brooklyn a decade later, you'd find Australians (or locals who've spent time in Australia) running awesome cafes serving up flat whites, piccolos, magics (ask someone from Melbourne) and avocado on toast. Not far away you'll probably find an Aesop store (anyone who has worked at Four Pillars knows my deep admiration for Aesop and how they've taken Melbourne's love of design, creativity, sustainability and quality to the world; more on Aesop on page 161). This idea of modern Australia as a progressive place of flavour, creativity, design, innovation, diversity and sustainability was an idea we wanted to be part of sharing.

The fourth and final piece (did I mention we like things in fours?) was thinking about what kind of business we wanted to be, what kind of impact we wanted to have on the world. And this went to the heart of what we believed modern business was all about: making something exceptional while also making a positive impact on the people and the places around you. So, we committed to supporting the communities our craft depended on. This was always the broadest and vaguest pillar of our purpose. What it meant to us was simply being good people and doing the right thing by everyone from our suppliers and customers to our local community and employees.

Here's how we wrote our purpose in our first strategy documents (and amazingly it has never changed):

We are Four Pillars Gin.

We are modern Australian makers of Gin.

Our purpose is to:

Elevate the CRAFT of distilling gin.

Celebrate the CRAFT of the cocktail.

Share the CRAFT of modern Australia.

Support the communities our CRAFT depends on.

The clunky capitalisation of CRAFT was always there four times whenever we wrote down our purpose, and it talked to the other key piece of the puzzle for us: the thing that was going to give us the right to succeed and to deliver on this purpose.

The world doesn't need another anything, but there's always room for a better something. That thought helped to give us clarity early on. The only way we were going to succeed was by making the best gin we could, and that would mean committing entirely to only making gin and committing entirely to placing product excellence before anything else (including profitability). The first, most important and only question was: What will it take to make better gin? This, for us, was the craft mindset, the maker mindset, that became the key enabler of all the growth and opportunity that lay in front of us.

Every conversation I have had about Four Pillars for over a decade has soon found me saying one of these phrases:

We are craft gin-makers...

We are makers not marketers...

We always begin with gin...

Over the years, we've repeated the same few mantras to remind ourselves and everyone who works for and with us that the quality of the gin is everything. And it almost inevitably leads to a discussion when someone asks the question: What is *craft*?

For many people, craft always means small. There's something romantic about picturing the craft maker (whether they're making gin, beer, wine, shoes or furniture) in some tiny distillery/brewery/winery/atelier/workshop making microscopic batches of their deeply personal, rare, special, limited product.

But working at that kind of microscale brings challenges. Either your product is going to be extraordinarily expensive (which means you'll build a business catering to a tiny elite at best or, at worst, you'll simply go out of business as no one is willing to pay the prices you're charging) or your product is going to be small batch but fatally compromised in terms of quality and/or consistency.

We took a different view, and we refused to define craft by scale. Instead, we reflected, it was a mindset. Craft meant simply placing product excellence, and the mastery of process and making that goes into product excellence, above everything else. So, in theory, you could scale craft as much as you wanted without any compromise in quality (which is critical if you're going to build trust, loyalty and perceptions of luxury... we'll discuss that later). It just so happens that the all-too-common view is that, as businesses grow, they tend to look for efficiencies and cost savings, and somewhere along the way the craft ethos and the uncompromising commitment to quality gets left behind.

So, we resolved to do things differently—to do 'craft at scale'. And the ambition that emerged during our first 18 months was to attempt to become the benchmark for craft gin at scale. Arguably, ten years on, we've achieved that ambition in Australia, but we still have a planet to conquer with our craft-at-scale gin movement.

USEFUL BIT #2:
THE BUTTERFLY
AND THE BRICK

Here's a question I always like to ask, not because I'm trying to get all philosophical and existential, but because I want to help you get to the heart of what your business is all about.

Why do you exist?

Or to put it another way:

Why do you matter? Why do your customers value you? Why would they mourn you if your business ceased to exist? And what is it about how you do things that makes all this possible?

In a perfect world, this thinking would be done before you make that first decision, but most of us don't live in a perfect world. Instead, most of us live in a world where the decision has been made, the business is up and running, and now we have the opportunity (and an urgent need) to think a bit more clearly about *why* we're doing what we're doing and *how* we're going to be successful.

There's very little that's original about the strategic planning tools and models I use. They're an amalgam of things I have heard, read and picked up along the way in my career. Two of the most useful models over the past 15 years have been the butterfly and the brick, particularly when used in concert with each other.

The butterfly

The butterfly model helps you think about the value you create in the world. It's a simple Venn diagram, where one wing asks 'What does the world need?' and the other asks 'What's special about you?' The magic of this simple (and deliberately simplistic) construct is in how it forces you to confront the risks of building a plan outside of the overlap at the heart of the butterfly.

38

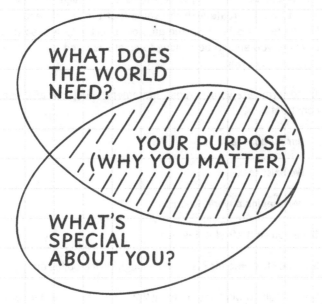

WHAT DOES
THE WORLD
NEED?

YOUR PURPOSE
(WHY YOU MATTER)

WHAT'S
SPECIAL
ABOUT YOU?

Create something that only speaks to what's special about you and you're at risk of what an Australian political campaigner I once worked with would have called a 'piss in a wetsuit'—a wonderfully vivid description for something that makes you feel warm but no one else notices.

Create something that only addresses what the world needs and you risk acting on a universal insight but without any right to succeed or win. Others will likely have a greater right than you to succeed in that insight territory.

The power of the butterfly is forcing you to align the value you're able to create with the value that the world needs to be created. This is where the area of opportunity lies, so this is where you should be looking to crystallise and define your purpose, your *why*.

Try to formulate your purpose statement using one of these constructs:

> *Our purpose is to....*

> *We exist to...*

> *We imagine a world where...*

Once you've drafted it, test it.

Is it true? Is it credible? Is it bold enough? Is it credible enough?

Does it talk to what you do today? Will it motivate and inspire what you could do tomorrow?

Does it give you room to grow? Does it address a real customer need? Does it create value? Will it inspire you to create irreplaceable value that your customer can't get from anyone else?

Could you be bolder? Do you need to be more specific and crunchy?

Remember, this is more than just a social purpose. This is your overarching reason for existing. It can't be too lofty; it needs to be specific to you. It needs to help you make decisions, maintain your focus, choose your priorities. But, equally, it can't be too everyday and short term. It should be timeless and should outlive your medium-term ambitions and visions. Your purpose is something that is never achieved, but instead continues to guide, focus and inspire you as the world changes and demands new things from you.

The brick

I've been obsessed with the power of the Lego brick ever since I saw Lego's former CEO Jørgen Vig Knudstorp talk about reconnecting Lego with its core purpose and placing the brick back at the centre of Lego's plans.

What Knudstorp realised (at a time when the world was becoming increasingly digital) was that Lego was in the business of brick-making, because the physical brick (and how two bricks fitted so perfectly together) was its source of true differentiation. All sorts of implications flowed from there, from the need to lead in moulding techniques to the need to master an enormously vast global inventory of billions of bricks.

If thinking about the butterfly helps you make sure that the value you want to create as a business (or any kind of organisation) is aligned with something the world values, then thinking about the brick helps you focus on what exactly you do (and need to do) to create that value. So in Lego's case, the butterfly anchors Lego in a world of play and limitless creativity, while the brick highlights that it's literally their Lego brick that gives them the unique right to be successful in that world of creative play. Between them, the butterfly and the brick can help you unlock a deeper understanding of the system you're trying to grow.

What's your brick? What's the differentiated source of value that sits at the heart of your ability to deliver on your purpose? If your purpose is your WHY, what's your HOW?

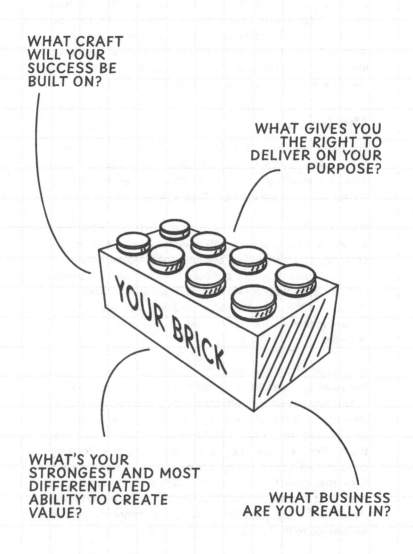

WHAT CRAFT
WILL YOUR
SUCCESS BE
BUILT ON?

WHAT GIVES YOU
THE RIGHT TO
DELIVER ON YOUR
PURPOSE?

YOUR BRICK

WHAT'S YOUR
STRONGEST AND MOST
DIFFERENTIATED
ABILITY TO CREATE
VALUE?

WHAT BUSINESS
ARE YOU REALLY IN?

Another way to think about the brick is that it helps you reflect on what business you're really in. Take Amazon. It's a retailer, but the business it's really in is friction removal. Amazon's model is to make it easier and easier for you to find, purchase and receive whatever you want. It's in the business of ease, efficiency and effortlessness. So, given the choice between making something sexier or making it simpler, you know what Amazon would choose every time. And, given the choice between spending on advertising or on enabling better customer experiences, again, you know which would be the right choice for Amazon.

No other retailer would have developed cloud computing to such a level that it ended up spinning off a standalone business, but Amazon did exactly that with Amazon Web Services. And it made sense because cloud computing power was at the heart of Amazon's drive for friction removal.

I hope interrogating and understanding your *why*, your *how* and the business you're *really* in will unlock new clarity for you, both on what matters most today (where you need to focus your efforts) and on which bets and opportunities are most appropriate to focus on in the future, helping you back yourself to make the right decisions and stay the course.

In some cases, doing this work may help you realise that there isn't enough there, and that you need to think again about the purpose and positioning of your business. That's hard medicine to swallow, but better to take it now than later.

Either way, onwards we go.

SIX

Growth theory, relationships and money

In Chapter 7, I'll talk about the branding decisions we made, but first, the last two foundational pieces. How were we going to grow this gin business of ours? And how were we going to pay for it all?

The three of us were each going to put significant cash into the business ourselves (we all agreed we could dig around and find $125 000 to invest, but that was very much the limit for each of us), but there was no question that we would need other investment. The debate was really about how much we would need and how much we were willing to dilute our own equity stakes in the business.

Ultimately, we all aligned around the belief that we would rather own a smaller stake in a business with deeper pockets (after all, doing everything properly and to the standards we were setting ourselves meant it would be a cash-hungry business for at least two years), so we agreed that we would hold 60 per cent of the equity for the three of us, and that we would seek 20 investors to take a 2 per cent stake each for $25 000. These 2 per cent stakes would come with no voting rights, so we would retain full control of the business, and we would now have $875 000 of start-up cash in the bank to play with. We valued the business at this stage at $1.25 million, comprising the cash we'd all put in plus the 'sweat' equity Cam, Stu and I committed to invest in the business (which we valued at $125 000 each, matching the cash we'd already put in with our time, effort and expertise).

Who did we choose to approach? We had two criteria, both borne from the same mindset: the three of us wanted to be able to build and run the business our way, so we didn't want to approach stressed or impatient money. We hadn't even made any gin yet, so we couldn't ask people to take too much risk. We didn't want anyone putting their life savings in the business or putting their homes on the line. Equally, we needed time to build a gin business our way, so we didn't want to invite investors who would be impatiently interrogating and scrutinising our every decision and short-term result. We were determined to play the long game.

We felt we probably (okay, hopefully) knew more about building a drinks brand than most of the people who would invest in us, so we wanted people who would enjoy the ride, but who would, for the most part, let us get on with steering the ship. Amazingly, that's how it worked out, with the bonus that our Ginvestors also offered huge support for our business through their generosity and enthusiasm, ordering, drinking, recommending and gifting our gin to everyone they met — and some also offered us access to their priceless professional expertise. But above all, they were brilliantly supportive friends, and our annual Ginvestor brief/dinner was always one of the highlights of the year.

Despite our excitement and our belief in the opportunity, the reality is that the initial uptake on the Ginvestor offer was relatively slow. Plenty of people responded politely but never followed up on the chance to discuss it further. A few others sent back respectful notes saying that they applauded the ambition but couldn't see how there was anything truly differentiated or compelling in what we were looking to do.

In hindsight, I realise that they couldn't see something that, in all honesty, we three founders didn't realise at the time—that the real differentiator was us, not simply as individuals, but as a trio. It was our complementary skillsets, experiences and relationships that gave us a disproportionate right to succeed. But we didn't realise that back then, so we couldn't expect the average investor to see it.

The result was that, by the time we launched our Pozible campaign (making us one of the first alcohol brands in the world to launch through crowdfunding), we had just nine of the 20 Ginvestor slots filled. A week later, after our Pozible campaign had gone supernova, we had 19 of them filled, and were receiving panicky emails from friends about keeping that twentieth slot open for them. What happened? In short, we crafted and launched a brand.

USEFUL BIT #3:
PICTURING SUCCESS

What you're doing, why you're doing it, how you're going to get it done. These are all critical questions to have clarity on. And now here are three more questions you need to reflect on as you begin your journey (or reflect on the next stage of a journey you've already begun)...

What do you picture when you picture success?

How are you going to achieve the growth that success requires?

What's stopping others from beating you to it?

If your first decision is about *what* you're going to do, and then the butterfly and the brick help you think about your *why* and your *how*, this last primary thinking exercise is about *where* you want to do it and the system you'll need to build to get you there.

Over the past two decades, I have run countless strategic planning workshops, and one area that trips people up is distinguishing between their purpose, mission, vision and ambition. To be frank, I don't really care what names you use, as long as you're clear on what you're trying to define.

If your purpose is timeless, then you need a time-bound ambition, a sense of where your purpose can take you. This is what the cover story can help you reflect on.

WHAT
MAGAZINE
(OR WEBSITE)
ARE YOU ON?

WHAT
DOES THE
HEADLINE
SAY?

MAJOR
MAGAZINE

YOUR
BUSINESS
STORY HERE

AND
HERE

AND
HERE
TOO

DO YOU HAVE A
NARRATIVE OF
SUCCESS FOR
YOUR BUSINESS?

ARE YOU ALIGNED
AROUND WHAT
SUCCESS LOOKS LIKE?

Picture your business on the cover of a major magazine. Picture your business success story on the homepage of a global website. Picture being interviewed as the featured guest on *Diary of a CEO* or *Acquired* podcast. Imagine your business as a *Harvard Business Review* case study—whatever floats your boat and helps you visualise that future state of success.

What's the story? What's the headline? What has your business done or achieved to deserve that focus and attention? Is it the ultimate expression of your purpose in action, the potential of your purpose and craft fulfilled? If so, then that's your cover story.

Your cover story (and remember, there are no rules here, so you may end up with two or three of them) should feel motivating and directional.

So, once you're clear on it, make sure your team, your partners and your investors all understand and share that ambition too. Nothing will test your partnership more over time than failing to recognise that the key actors in your business have very different ideas about why you're doing this, where you're heading and how you're going to get there.

Talking of how you're going to get there, your cover story should also help you think through your business system and how it will enable that success. If that's your picture of success, what decisions or actions will get you there?

The trick is to work backwards from the achievement of the cover story. One way to do that is to use the 5 Whys method of interrogation.

The idea of asking 'why?' five times is a common diagnostic tool typically used to expose the underlying problems in a situation (e.g. The car crashed because the wheel came off. Why? The wheel came off because the bolt came loose. Why? The bolt came loose because the bolt tightening tool was faulty. Why? The tool was fault because it wasn't maintained properly. Why? We don't have the right procedures in place for maintenance, training and safety checks... You get the picture). The point being that every time we ask 'why?' we get closer to the true, underlying causes and drivers.

In this case, try using the same process of causal interrogation but for a positive outcome. We achieved our ambition. Why? Because we did these things. Why did those things work? Why were we able to do those things? Again, you get the picture.

What we're trying to get to here is a sense of what must have happened. How has your business had to perform and scale to achieve your ambition? By working backwards, you can start to develop the growth theory that will, in turn, now propel your company forwards. What will be the most important drivers of your growth and success, and how will they then interact and interconnect? This is at the heart of your growth theory.

Lastly, if your growth theory is about playing offence, what will give your business a strong defence? What will prevent others from easily replicating your model and chasing down that same ambition?

The legendary investor Warren Buffet talks about the idea of businesses having a moat around them. What makes your moat wide (with lots of hard-to-replicate advantages) or deep (with one utterly differentiating advantage)?

Ideally your moat will be wide and deep. But be honest and critical as you consider what makes your moat compelling. Do you need to dig a deeper, wider moat before you start to chase down that cover story?

For a business like Uber, their moat is single-mindedly about scale (it's narrow but deep). The scale of their fleets of drivers in each city they operate in (ferrying both passengers and deliveries) gives them an extremely hard-to-replicate advantage. For a business like Hermès, the moat is arguably much more multidimensional (it's wider and more diverse), from their craft training centres to their ateliers (fancy workshops) to their brand and heritage to their iconic bags and scarves to their bricks-and-mortar stores. In both cases, these deep or wide moats represent a hard-to-cross, hard-to-replicate advantage over your competitors.

CAN YOUR
MOAT BE
DEEPER OR
WIDER?

YOUR MOAT

YOUR MOAT

ARE YOUR
ADVANTAGES
FOCUSED OR
DIVERSE?

USEFUL BIT #4:
THINKING IN ACTION: A FOUR PILLARS EXAMPLE

Having worked through the first three Useful Bits of this book with your ambitions in mind, I thought it would be useful to have a look at how we used some of these models and thought processes to think about the journey Four Pillars was embarking on back in 2013. I've also included some of the actual artefacts of our Four Pillars thinking journey so they won't line up perfectly with my models (instead they are authentic documents of what we committed ourselves to).

This first example shows how we thought about our purpose, our craft and what business we're really in (the first inspired by the butterfly, the latter two inspired by the brick from page 38).

At Four Pillars, we cheated by giving ourselves four strands (or pillars) to our purpose, but the first (elevate the craft of gin-distilling) was always the critical one. And we knew that our brick was always going to be our total commitment to and obsession with our gin craft, our maker DNA, our commitment to what we called Ginnovation (for about a week, then we got sick of the play on words). We were in the business of obsessing about, exploring and amplifying the craft of making gin in a modern Australian way—nothing more, nothing less.

Our responses to the butterfly and the brick weren't rocket science, but they were highly effective at focusing us and helping us make decisions fast and with great confidence in our early years. The results of this thinking showed up in the form of our purpose, our commitment to our craft DNA and our clarity over what business we were really in. You don't need your responses to be rocket science either; they just need to be true, motivating and useful.

WHAT BUSINESS ARE WE IN?	WE ARE MODERN AUSTRALIAN MAKERS OF GIN
WHAT'S OUR CRAFT AND DNA?	AN AGILE, HIGHLY-CREATIVE CRAFT-DRIVEN BUSINESS WITH A PASSION FOR BEING MAKERS, NOT MARKETERS
WHAT'S OUR PURPOSE?	ELEVATE THE CRAFT OF GIN DISTILLING CELEBRATE THE CRAFT OF COCKTAILS SHARE THE CRAFT OF MOD OZ

SUPPORT THE COMMUNITY OUR CRAFT DEPENDS ON

Motivating, that is, to us. We took the view that, with a few notable exceptions, our customers probably don't care about our purpose, but they do care deeply about what our purpose inspired us to create for them. You might come to the same conclusion. If so, think of your purpose as a tool for strategy and decision making, maybe the most important one you have. Just don't assume that drafting a compelling purpose will give anyone a reason to purchase your product.

That leads nicely to our ambition, working model and growth theory.

We wanted to set a new benchmark for craft gin globally. Drafting that ambition forced us to have a point of view on craft (that it was about quality, not smallness) and on our geographic ambitions (we wanted to win at home first, but not limit ourselves to our home market). So we defined our ambition as:

Our ambition is to be the new benchmark for craft gin on a global scale.

We also wanted to think differently about how to lead a business like this, not just in the form of our co-CEO model, but also in terms of what the key roles and functions should be. We agreed that we would lead the business together, visualising the business as a triangle with each focused on giving our business an edge (with many of the conventional functions of a business sitting at the intersections of those edges). Cameron took the lead on giving us a distilling and operational edge; Stu took the lead on giving us a trade and relationships edge; and I took the lead on giving us a brand and community edge.

We believed we would achieve our ambitions by building a business led by craft, powered by a culture that valued making, and amplified by a social-first brand that focused on craft intimacy. At first, we did most of this instinctively, but as we grew we started to formalise (and write down) our understanding of what was driving, and would continue to drive, our growth.

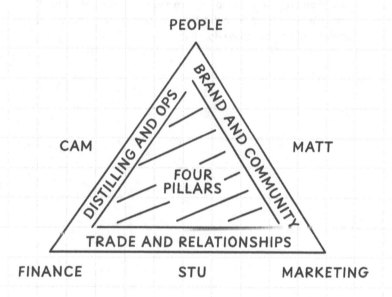

PEOPLE

CAM

MATT

FINANCE

STU

MARKETING

Lastly, how would all of this add up to putting a wide and deep moat around our business? Or, to put it in the words of our Ginvestors: what's stopping anyone else from making gin in a similar style and fast following everything you're doing?

The answer we came up with was that it was a combination of factors, all anchored in our absolute focus on gin and our maker DNA. It was a long list, which perhaps reinforces why running Four Pillars has always felt both energising and a little overwhelming. But, ultimately, it was proven entirely correct. The way we chose to build this gin business of ours was something only we could do.

✳ 1. A CRAFT-LED BUSINESS

~~CRAFT = SLOW AND SMALL~~
~~CRAFT = WANKY AND OVERSERIOUS~~
~~CRAFT = FAST AND SCALABLE~~
CRAFT = INCLUSIVE AND FUN

✳ 2. A FOCUS ON MAKING, NOT MARKETING

~~MAKING = A DISTILLERY PHILOSOPHY~~
MAKING = A WHOLE-OF-BUSINESS
PHILOSOPHY. A BELIEF IN EARNING
MEDIA, NOT PAYING FOR IT

✳ 3. A SOCIAL BRAND BUILT ON CRAFT INTIMACY

~~SOCIAL = A PUSH COMMUNICATION CHANNEL~~
SOCIAL = AN ENABLER OF DIGITAL INTIMACY
AND AMPLIFIER OF PHYSICALLY INTIMATE
EXPERIENCES

THE FOUR
PILLARS
MOAT

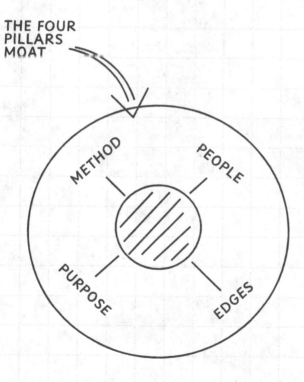

PART TWO

Crafting

SEVEN

Rare Dry Gin and the crafting of the Four Pillars brand

We couldn't keep talking about our purpose, our ambition and our craft mindset forever (Stu would have killed me). At some stage we needed to start working on what we were going to launch. And, with Wilma the still not yet in the Yarra Valley, that work took two forms. With Cameron in his *Breaking Bad* phase playing with botanicals down in Victoria, up in New South Wales, Stu, my wife Rebecca (who would go on to build all our brand and marketing capabilities for the first five years) and I were putting together the brief for the initial brand design work.

The irony of how we went about crafting Four Pillars is that, while we have always been about the gin first and foremost, we were actually developing our initial brand designs and packaging in parallel with Cam developing the gin. So, we were designing an idea of what we wanted the Four Pillars brand to represent even though we didn't have the final recipe for Rare Dry Gin yet.

In other words, we were starting to think both about the product that would define Four Pillars and the literal and figurative packaging we wanted to place around that product. We were starting the long journey of crafting a story, an image and, yes, a brand. We approached this work with a clear sense of philosophy and belief that has only gotten stronger over the decade that has followed.

My brand education had begun years earlier. Long before I was drinking and disliking gin, I was a kid growing up in Cyprus drinking gallons of soft drink (don't judge me, it was the 1980s; it was 36 degrees in the shade; and I was a pale-skinned, freckled kid from Britain). My parents moved to Cyprus when I was three, and I had eight joyous years growing up there, and it was where my first brand preferences were formed: Manchester United, 7-Up and Mirinda (never Sprite or Fanta), Le Coq Sportif (random, I know), Aiwa (my Aiwa Walkman was my prized possession), Duran Duran, Sharp (they were Manchester United's shirt sponsor) and British Airways (back when you could sit in the cockpit mid-flight).

Why did eight-year-old me feel so strongly about being a Manchester United fan, and not a Liverpool fan, having never visited either city? Why was I so drawn to Aiwa and not Sony, the parent brand. Or why did some of the brand preferences I formed at that time fade fast (looking at you, Le Coq Sportif), while others have held firm for 40 years (I still have a deep-seated affection for British Airways, despite my too-frequent disappointment when I fly with them). Or why did I instinctively make East London my home when I first moved to London in 1997, despite my best friends all living out West, and why did I never feel entirely comfortable journeying too far north or south.

None of these choices or preferences are entirely rational. But they were mine and they quickly formed part of my identity. And here's the big spoiler for the rest of this book: none of our brand biases are ever fully predictable or fully rational. They are formed and influenced by a combination of serendipity, distribution, availability, emotion, association, design, aesthetics, experiences, memories and stories (told both to us and by us).

Brands, in short, do not exist. Real things exist—banks, airlines, trainers, gins, cities, celebrities, political parties—and we all have feelings about these things. We can rationalise these feelings, but they are not in themselves rational. *Brand* is just a word we use to describe the sum total of these feelings, these biases, towards a business. When enough people have the same strong, positive feelings and biases towards a business, you've got a strong brand on your hands.

A brand is not its branding (the visual identity of a business), although strong branding can help shape how people feel about your business. At the end of the day, brand is just bias. And even the most dry, work-like business can benefit from its customers, clients, stakeholders and employees having stronger, more positive emotions and biases around it.

That's all fine in theory, but here I was facing the reality of my first opportunity to help hardwire bias and emotion into my own business. The majority of that bias would come from the quality of the product and the power of the experiences we curated for people. But all of that was to come in the future. For now, the remit was strictly design and storytelling. We needed a bottle, a label, a story. We had the chance to influence people's first impressions of this new gin from Australia.

As we'd made clear in our investor memorandum, Four Pillars was a real business, a gin distillery, and it would be driven by a commitment to craft and making (not marketing). But around that craft-led maker business, we would have the chance to create a brand with real meaning, appeal, resonance and longevity. After years of working in politics and then brand agencies advising others, here was my chance to take my own medicine, and put into practice the theories I'd been developing for a decade.

Where do you even begin? Simply put, we started with the basic necessities. We needed a bottle, and we all agreed that you only got one chance to be original, so we wanted a bottle that was custom and unique to our business. It was an expensive decision (another driver of that decision to invite investors into our business from day one), but we knew that our future customers would form much of their sense of what Four Pillars was about and whether it was for them simply by holding the bottle in their hand. If the bottle didn't perform, then the gin would never get a chance to shine. Context, as much as content, is king for brands, and our bottle was the first bit of context we would get to control.

We needed a label to put on the bottle, and that meant we needed a name to put on the label, plus a story to go on the side of the label.

And, soon, we would need the beginnings of a playbook to help us make other decisions, from designing our six-pack cases to thinking about our website. We all had plenty of thoughts to contribute, but we would need a design agency with packaging experience to make sense of our ideas. A friend referred me to an agency called WAR and we got to work.

First up was the bottle. Along with selecting our still (Wilma) and our gin botanicals (a work in progress as we awaited Wilma's arrival), choosing a bottle felt like the next most substantial decision we would make. The bottle was literally how people (both bartenders and drinkers) would pick up and hold our brand. If it didn't feel right in their hands, it might never make it to their mouths.

We talked a lot about what kind of brand we wanted to be. At the time, there were lots of new gin brands being launched overseas (the Australian craft gin boom was still to come) and some were leaning into their newness with radically modern bottles. WAR explored options for a bottle shape that would feel really disruptive and new, but we feared that something too '2013' could start to feel tired within a few years. That helped us realise that a timeless sense of quality was a critical part of the brand we wanted to create.

Equally, we had no desire to create something with fake heritage, so we didn't need to mimic the gin bottles of the past and pretend to hark back to London in the 1700s. In fact, it was a couple of tequila bottles that provided the closest inspiration for the beautiful custom bottle shape we ended up landing on.

Stu led the charge with bartenders, peppering them with questions about bottles they liked or didn't like and showing them early mock-ups of our proposed bottle. We learned that a shorter bottle was favoured (more stable and hefty in the hand), but not too wide, so even someone with smaller hands could comfortably pick it up and pour with one hand. And the neck should be long enough to make it easy to pour a shot without dribbling at the end (something multiple bartenders told us frustrated them about the very stubby neck on the Hendrick's bottle).

In parallel with this work on the bottle, the WAR team started working on the label design. Again, they pushed at the edges of our brief, showing us things that were both super contemporary and more traditional. And, again, we aimed to strike that balance of timeless, crafted luxury—not too modern or sterile, but also not too retro, fancy or projecting fake heritage. We wanted something clearly premium, but also restrained and not over the top.

Lastly, we needed a name to put on all this design work. Over my years as a brand strategist and consultant, naming has always been my least favourite part of the job. In short, there are no good names, but there are bad ones. So, avoid bad names, and make your name a good one.

LG is not (in my opinion, at least) a good name. It's short for Lucky Goldstar (although few people realise that anymore), which is a bad name (hence why LG have been happy to allow people to forget its original meaning). So Lucky Goldstar was shortened to LG, and the brand was then given meaning through decades of brand campaigns proclaiming that 'Life's Good'. So many great businesses have names that started out clunky like 'Facebook' (a compound name, originally prefaced with a clumsy 'The'), a bit random like 'Google' (a very big number), rather obscure like 'Tesla' (a dead, famous-ish scientist) or, in the case of the Australian unicorn Canva, needing a full rethink (Canva was a French-inspired pivot from its previous, and objectively terrible, name Canvas Chef). In all cases, the key was not the name, but the meaning built into the name over time.

The not terrible name we came up with was 'Four Pillars'. That was Stu's proposal when we needed something to go into the initial design mock-ups and it stuck. What does it mean? Well, it depends on who you ask (there's a non-sanctioned and inappropriate version Stu is liable to tell after a few Negronis). The official story is that Four Pillars refers to our belief in the need to focus on doing a few things (ideally four things) to an exceptional standard. It's a belief in focus, excellence and simplicity, like the world's greatest cocktail, the Negroni (equal parts gin, Campari, sweet vermouth and good ice, see page 142 for some more inspiration for this drink). We added the word 'gin' to the end, making the official brand name Four Pillars Gin, emphasising our absolute focus on the craft of making gin and only gin.

As we developed the brand, we started to use this idea of four pillars of focus and excellence to describe what went into each gin. For example, the four pillars of our first signature release, Rare Dry Gin, were a great still, the best botanicals, pure water and our love of the craft of distilling.

The last piece of the brand puzzle was to agree on colours. Gin was dominated by blues (Bombay Sapphire), greens (Tanqueray) and reds (Gordon's, Beefeater). The outlier was Hendrick's with its almost medicinal dark black bottle. As we were looking to compete with Hendrick's at the top end of the price bracket (over AU$70 a bottle), we wanted to pick colours that communicated status, premium and (again) timelessness.

The end result was our iconic black label with copper foil. When lit from the front, the bottle looked stunning. When backlit, the light would cause the black label to grey out and the copper to become almost unreadable. This was a choice that caused us pain for years until our long-term design partners, Weave, identified new label stocks and printing techniques that could give us the finish and look we wanted while also blocking out light and ensuing great readability.

I'm so glad we held our nerve on all those decisions, from sticking with the black label (despite some people saying that gin was a summer drink and black was too dark, heavy and wintery) to sticking with the name Four Pillars (despite someone warning us that the number four was unlucky in Chinese) to making the big investment to have a custom-moulded bottle from the outset (despite the minimal order soaking up far too much of our limited cash to purchase glass we wouldn't need for ages). Because the truth is that, while so much about our brand has evolved and grown since those initial design explorations with WAR in 2013, our core Rare Dry Gin bottle has remained broadly untouched and already feels like an icon on the world gin scene.

The finishing touch that made it feel so iconic? The WAR team came up with a simple brand motif of four dots (as if looking down at four pillars from above) and we thought it would be beautiful if those four dots could be moulded into the glass. We took advantage of having a custom mould made for the bottles, and we placed the four dots proudly on the glass, a wonderfully tactile demonstration of the brand's attention to detail and sense of quality, its premium feel and distinction.

I knew we had created something special years later when a restaurateur in Melbourne called me out of the blue asking if they could get hold of 100 empty bottles to use as water bottles for their new venue opening. They wanted a beautiful bottle to use for water at every table and the best option they could think of was our iconic gin bottle.

Not everything was a home run. The choice of a black label meant our bottle and brand could look a bit dark and gloomy in the wrong light or environment. But, in return for that decision, we got ourselves a label (and a brand) that looked spectacular when photographed well. This connected the dots to our emerging theory of growth—that we would build a brand through craft intimacy, encouraging a hands-on experience with our Distillery, our gin and our drinks whenever possible; and we would scale that intimacy through beautiful photography, film (once we had the budget to start making high-quality videos) and storytelling. I coined the phrase 'phygital intimacy' to describe this approach of harnessing both physical and digital experiences, a phrase that never fails to inspire schoolboy sniggering and mockery from Cam and Stu (they keep me #grounded).

The first hero shoot for the brand (with the amazing photographer Anson Smart) took place in Stu's dining room and utilised dummy bottles full of water. We were trying to build emotion and resonance around a gin that didn't exist, and we had to write side-label copy for a gin recipe that hadn't yet been finalised. But luckily, in August 2013, Wilma arrived and, within a week, Cam and his great mates Flammo and Hally had put her together, got her working and we were on our way to our first properly made gin samples.

Just as the crafting of our brand's design language was a question of nuance, the same was true for the gin. We wanted to create a distinctly modern Australian take on gin, and we agreed that modern Australian flavours were defined by our love for Mediterranean citrus and freshness combined with our love for Asian spice and heat. All that said, we wanted to make something that worked brilliantly in the three core classic gin drinks—a G&T, a Martini and a Negroni—so Cam couldn't stray too far from gin convention.

In the end, after experimenting with botanicals for the best part of 18 months, we settled on nine dry botanicals—a pretty equal mix of local and exotic. The local botanicals included Tasmanian pepper berry and lemon myrtle (the latter being the botanical that continues to put Australian gin on the world gin map); the exotics included juniper (of course), cardamom, star anise and coriander seeds. But, perhaps most interesting was the final ingredient, our use of whole oranges, which is highly unusual, but made a great complement to the spicier botanicals like coriander, cardamom and star anise.

The gin (we called it Rare Dry Gin because we reckon it's a rare take on classic 'dry' gin) was clearly special, in part thanks to Cam's and Stu's instincts around botanicals and flavour, and in part due to the quality of the still we had commissioned. Like all CARL stills, she is uniquely good at both purifying the spirit (giving us a super smooth gin) and concentrating flavour (giving us a gin full of big, bold flavours and aromas).

Over the course of six months we had crafted a gin and the foundations of a brand identity that have stood the test of time. The work we did at that stage remains a benchmark for everything that has followed. Were we lucky or were we reaping the benefits of having thought so clearly about what we were trying to do? A bit of both probably.

Ultimately, it comes back to decisions. Small details and small actions that added up to a big impact. The small decisions included crafting a neck tag for every bottle of Rare Dry Gin that communicated both the still name (even though, at this time, we only had one), the batch number and the bottle number. All of these small details signalled the craft and attention to detail we wanted people to feel when they held that bottle in their hands. Another small decision was to add personality to the reminders to drink responsibly, so in addition to the mandatory words and logos, we added the phrase: 'Don't drink more, drink better'. This helped to embed a sense of personality and philosophy in the brand, something for the drinker to discover deep within the fine print of the label. Everything communicates.

Meanwhile, this was a period of frenetic action, not just decisions. On 9 October 2013, we had our first label run booked in at the printers. Rebecca was there to help select the final foil colour in real time. On the same day, we finally received our permit from the Australian Tax Office to make gin. It wasn't until 11 November that Cameron was able to send samples of the final gin up to Sydney for me and Stu to taste. Less than a month before the gin's public debut and Cam was like a great chef, still perfecting the final recipe, and debating with Stu about the exact amount of star anise to use.

USEFUL BIT #5:
CAPABILITIES, BEHAVIOURS AND RELATIONSHIPS

When you move from the thinking phase to the crafting phase of your business, everything starts happening fast. This is where the clichés start flying, the rubber hits the road and shit gets real.

You need to take a moment and ask yourself (honestly):

Do you have the stuff you need?

I'll be honest, this next tool isn't one that we used when building Four Pillars. Fortunately for us, the combination of our founding group of six (me, Stu and Cam plus our three wives Rebecca, Sally and Leah, all brilliantly talented professionals and experts in their fields), plus the friends, collaborators, supporters and early hires we made meant that we had most of the bases covered. Critically, our collective experience served us well as we made these decisions mostly based on gut instinct.

Nonetheless, if I was doing it all again, I would think it through a bit like this.

First, take the growth theory from the thinking phase (page 45), and break it down into the key drivers of your growth. What are the things you're going to need to do to deliver on your overarching ambition? What does your growth tell you about what will drive your success? At the heart of the answer for Four Pillars was that our craft-led ambition meant we needed to own every step of world-class gin production, starting with the best still and equipment we could find. This was a 'fact' that was baked in to every plan from day one.

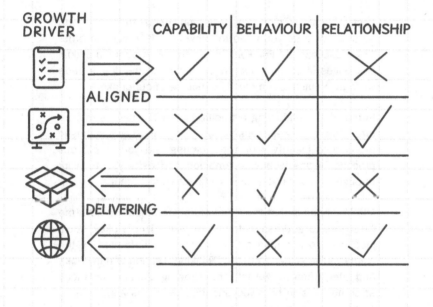

GROWTH DRIVER		CAPABILITY	BEHAVIOUR	RELATIONSHIP
	ALIGNED	✓	✓	✗
		✗	✓	✓
	DELIVERING	✗	✓	✗
		✓	✗	✓

Second, for each of those major growth drivers, what capability will you need to have, acquire, borrow or build? For Four Pillars and our belief in craft intimacy and the importance of building brand bias around our craft, this meant building our core creative marketing capabilities in-house and not outsourcing the telling of our story to third-party agencies.

Third, what culture will you need to foster? What behaviours will you need to encourage and enable? For Four Pillars this was about fostering a quality-obsessed, maker-led mindset from day one.

Lastly, what relationships will you need to foster and nurture? Who do you need to know (and influence) in order to be successful? For Four Pillars this was about the dual challenges of building deep relationships in the drinks trade while also building community directly with our drinkers.

Rather than conducting a traditional SWOT analysis of your strengths and weaknesses, or using another diagnostic exercise to identify your opportunities and your gaps, this process begins with your ambition and asks you to work through (realistically) what it will take to realise that ambition.

The likelihood is that you'll find more gaps than you have the resources to address in the short term. That's okay. You'll just need to prioritise and trust your gut (informed by the clarity you've gained from the 'Thinking' section of this book). And later, when we get into the 'Growing' section, we'll look at some tools to help you prioritise decisions and areas of investment and focus.

For now, however, we've spent enough time on the rational side of your business. In the next Useful Bit on page 78, we'll look at the role of emotion as a growth driver. We're going to help your business define how it feels.

EIGHT

The first three months

By 15 October, it was all systems go on everything to do with our launch. With Stu focused on launching the brand to the media and the trade, Cameron on distilling and bottling and Rebecca on connecting the dots between everything, my focus was firmly on getting ready to launch our first Pozible campaign. Pozible was, at the time, the world's third-largest crowdfunding platform and the only one run out of Australia. It felt like a natural place to build our first community while Cameron was still fine-tuning the gin.

We knew the Pozible campaign was going to be a success within hours. Within a day, we were on the front page of the Pozible website, soon after we'd hit our target, and within four days we'd sold out our whole first batch. We had a great story, well told, with a compelling piece of storytelling on film from Stu and some sensational imagery thanks to Rebecca and Anson Smart. Backed by the support of friends, family and mates in the trade, and boosted by the extraordinary enthusiasm of gin drinkers we'd never met from around the country, we had got our brand off to a flying start.

We sold 420 bottles in just over 90 hours and raised just over $30000. We built the beginnings of our customer database, with 300 people who hadn't just clicked 'Like' on Facebook, but had actually handed over their cold hard cash and suggested they would do so again. And we now had a proof of concept, both for the demand for great Australian gin and for the power of social media, storytelling and word-of-mouth marketing.

By the start of December 2013, we had sold our first batch (and had recruited our Batch Number One Club of drinkers to whom we promised lifetime early access to every new gin we went on to make). Cam had finalised the recipe for Rare Dry Gin, and we were ready to share the gin with the trade, the media and the world at a series of events in great gin-forward bars from Melbourne's iconic Gin Palace to Sydney's The Rook (both of which would go on to play key roles in the development of future gins).

From these launch parties to private trade tastings to sending bottles to key drinks media, the response to Four Pillars and the final gin that Cameron made was extraordinary. Cameron's use of fresh citrus gave us a simple signature garnish for a G&T—a big, delicious wedge of orange. This was the contemporary, delicious, modern Australian gin and the perfect moreish G&T we had dreamed of creating, and the reception was overwhelming.

Following our first launch events in early December, Stu and Sally Lewis drew on all their relationships and know-how to make sure that everyone who mattered was tasting, talking about and writing about Four Pillars. A great example of the response was a piece by the wine and drinks writer and blogger Drew Lamber, published on 16 January 2014, where he asked, 'Can an Australian-made gin taste better than Hendrick's?' and noted that 'Gin is supposed to be British, and more importantly, from London! Right?' Wrong, he decided, declaring Four Pillars the 'clear favourite' in his blind tests against Hendrick's and Bombay Sapphire, referring to Four Pillars as a 'Hendrick's Killer'.

So, yes, we were a tiny player going against the gins of some of the biggest booze multinationals on the planet. And, yes, we had a tiny marketing budget. And, yes, we could only make 400 bottles of gin at a time. But the early signs were good. This was working. Momentum was building. Pozible customers were reordering. Local bars and restaurants wanted to stock us. Dan Murphy's not only took the meeting, but they ranged the gin. Our theories were working. We had:

- a world-class gin, but with a modern Australian accent
- a brand with timeless luxury, quality cues, but a warm, friendly, inclusive, modern Australian tone of voice

- beautiful bespoke packaging
- small group trade engagement
- a social community building
- human faces (Stu's and Cam's, not mine!)
- a sense of being craft, small, quality obsessed and paying personal attention to every tiny detail
- a sense of higher purpose, helping to define a modern Australian distilling and, in particular, gin-distilling tradition.

Did it nearly go wrong at any stage? Looking back, it seems like there were surprisingly few moments of jeopardy. Like when the ship carrying our first delivery of custom bottles got stuck in the South China Sea and we made the expensive decision to airfreight enough glass to cover the first two batches, and then hoped the rest would arrive before all our momentum ran out.

But, in truth, the bigger risks were in the sliding doors moments, the things that didn't happen. For example, what if we hadn't run that crowdfunding campaign? Would we have generated the PR that we did, the excitement that we did and the Ginvestor demand that we did? Or what if we had decided that selling gin direct to consumers was likely to annoy the big retailers? Would we have created the consumer demand and excitement that then helped energise our initial retail sales?

The good news is we didn't walk through those sliding doors, and instead took the path we did. All of which meant that we now had the wind in our sails and confidence in our approach.

And it's just as well we ended 2013 with such confidence and conviction because the response to Rare Dry Gin and the launch of Four Pillars was beyond anything we could have hoped for, and we needed every ounce of focus and conviction we could muster to keep us on course. If 2013 had been a madcap rush to create and launch the world's best gin, the first few months of 2014 were about to take the madness to another level. Amid all that excitement, the first big challenge to our business also showed up in March 2014, and it took the form of the best possible news.

USEFUL BIT #6:
FEELING BENCHMARKS

This Useful Bit is a hard one for me to write, because the short story is that this is where I would always urge any business to engage professionals (unless you're fortunate enough to have people with the professional discipline and ability in your founding group, as we were).

But I hope that this Useful Bit at least helps you think about how to add a layer of emotion and design onto your business, ensuring that you value the feeling side of your business enough and know what questions to ask when you do engage some professional creative help.

The question here is:

How do you want your business to feel?

First, a bit of background. I studied economics at university, and economists like to think of perfectly operating markets full of rational actors. But this, it turns out, is far from the truth of the world we actually live in. In fact, the one branch of economics that gets it right is the one I didn't study at university: behavioural economics. The bit that begins with the understanding that behaviour isn't at all rational but is, in fact, highly influenced by all manner of unseen factors (sometimes known as nudges). Read anything by Daniel Kahneman or Richard Thaler to give yourself a better understanding of the discipline and its implications.

Here's the short story. The success of your business depends on people (duh!). Specifically, it depends on people making the decisions you need them to make: to choose your product, to recommend your business, to be loyal to you, to pay more for you, to work for you, to partner with you. And whatever decision they make, they will believe it's rational, but it's not. Every decision we make is driven by our emotions, our feelings and our biases. Which means that, even if we can

YOUR BRAND STORY

STORY
DEFINING ⟹ WHAT IS YOUR BRAND STORY? WHAT STORY DO YOU WANT TO TELL ABOUT YOUR BUSINESS?

STORY
DOING ⟹ WHAT ARE YOU DOING TO REFLECT THAT STORY IN YOUR BRAND'S ACTIONS? HOW DO YOUR BRAND'S EXPERIENCES REFLECT THIS?

STORY
TELLING ⟹ IS YOUR BUSINESS EFFECTIVELY TELLING YOUR STORY? DOES YOUR CUSTOMER KNOW AND UNDERSTAND IT?

post-rationalise them, every decision we make has a level of emotion and bias at the heart of it.

I've got a couple of side models for you to play with here, the first focused on your story (which we started to discuss in Useful Bit #3). We'll cover the detailed development of your messaging on page 102, but hopefully the thinking you've done already has helped you refine the story you would like to tell about your business, your product, your value and your purpose. This is the act of *storydefining*.

On page 130 we'll also look at how the most powerful form of storytelling is getting others to tell your story for you, and how that it is driven by the experiences you create and curate for them (which you could call *storydoing*).

But underpinning it all is the need to make sure that the story you've defined, the story you want to tell and the story you want others to experience and tell about you all matches up to the story your business tells and to how the business looks and feels. For example, if you want your business to tell a story of how your product enables wellbeing and athleticism, how does your business need to look? And, more importantly, how should your target audience feel when they come into contact with your business and its story?

This should help you start to define some benchmarks for how you need your business to feel. Or, to put it another way, what feelings are useful to your business?

When people interact with your business what do you want them to feel: trust, excitement, nostalgia, quality? Think about businesses you admire and trust. What feelings do you associate with them? Notice how they make conscious choices to evoke those feelings (I, for example, always notice the engineering that goes into small details in Apple stores like their staircases. It makes me feel that Apple cares deeply about design, engineering and attention to detail).

What signals do you want to send to people with your choices of language, colour, design and photography? You don't have to be the expert in these mediums (you can find and hire them), but you do need to own the brief, the intention. Your business is too important to leave these choices in the hands of creative people who lack your understanding of what you're creating or who you're creating it for.

Your brand has body language, which is conveyed in every choice you make. What do you want it to say? Are you making the most of every touchpoint, every chance to send a signal, every opportunity to shape how people feel about your business?

NINE

Overnight emails, opportunism and staying on strategy

As I've talked about, one of the most important differentiators for Four Pillars was the experience and abilities of the founders, both individually and collectively. If it was obvious what an Olympian with a great palate and Australia's best booze PR guy would bring to the party, it was less obvious what instincts and biases I would bring.

From day one, my career path has been somewhat unconventional. On face value, it's hard to see how I made the journey from British civil servant to Australian gin-maker, and from economic adviser to brand strategist, but at every stage, the leaps have made sense (to me, at least) and every experience has contributed to my ability to add value to the next situation.

This unconventional journey illustrates two things. First, where the perspective I brought to Four Pillars came from, and why I brought the baggage, biases and (arguably) expertise that I did. Second, that our whole careers and lives are just one long chain of sliding doors moments, the history of Four Pillars being no exception. How we navigate those sliding doors moments and how we join those dots comes down to a combination of good luck, good instincts and a good sense of what really drives you (whether we're talking about an individual career or a growing business).

'Adding value' was a mantra drummed into me by my father. Both my parents have had fascinating careers of their own, building on their initial professional foundations (my father as a civil engineer, my mother as a teacher) to succeed in new territories (as a CEO and an author, respectively). Both navigated significant change by holding onto the core of what they were good at and what gave them energy professionally. My dad was always very clear that the key was to understand and focus on the value you could add—in your job and in any room you found yourself in.

Now, while that may seem like a self-evident truth, there's a really powerful thought behind it. Knowing what value you can add, and committing to becoming better and more capable in that area, requires that you also understand what areas you should leave to others. Think of it as a personal application of the thought processes behind the butterfly and the brick (see page 38), helping you focus on deepening your areas of strength, and recognise the compatible and complementary skillsets of others whose strengths are well-matched with your areas of relative weakness.

So, what were my differentiating strengths? How did I add value? At first, I had no fixed idea. Maybe that's what has allowed me to keep walking through these sliding doors of opportunity and to make the most of what I found on the other side. My first job, straight out of university was in military intelligence. I had been recruited by the Government Economic Service, a specialist 'fast-stream' entry point for economics graduates into the UK civil service. And, while most of my fellow assistant economist newbies were placed in regular departments like health, education, transport and environment, I had been placed in the Defence Intelligence Staff, based in the Old

War Office in Whitehall in London. A year later, I moved to my second posting at the Treasury (the UK's finance ministry).

Those first two professional working years were a blur of desk research, meetings, memos covered in red pen by my frighteningly intelligent bosses and meetings with departments from across Whitehall. And during this time, I was starting to discover what I was good at: simplifying complexity, telling stories, mobilising language, persuading others. Without realising what was happening, the first 12 months of my working life shaped the next 12 years. Less than two years into my career as an economic adviser and I wasn't an economist at all. I was becoming a strategist and a communicator. I just didn't know it yet.

In 2001, I moved from the UK civil service into politics. Once again, I was offered a job as an analyst, this time joining the UK Conservative Party's newly formed Policy Unit. Within six months, I'd been poached to head up the Economic Section of the legendary Conservative Research Department (a training ground for future Tory cabinet ministers). Within a year, I was one of a small group writing the majority of the leader's speeches and crafting the party's political language and narrative.

This is not a book about my career, and I'm not the story here. But it's useful to reflect on the unconventional path I've taken to get to where I am today. How, from 1997 to 2005, I spent my time being good enough at the things I needed to be good enough at, while taking the opportunities to move into areas where I could use my strengths and excel. For me, my true strength was not in the things that really mattered (analysis, intelligence, policy, etc.) but in telling the stories of those things, making sense of those things and persuading others about those things.

If I were to fast-forward another decade, I would find the same thing happening at Four Pillars: the gin was the only thing that mattered, and I could add no real value there. My value, my contribution, was in telling the stories about the incredible gin. But first, I had one more decade to sharpen my skillset.

Along the way I had met a girl, Rebecca. The woman who would forever change the trajectory and geography of my life, not least because she was Australian. We met at a party in North London, had one date and then she flew home. By the time she'd landed back in Sydney, she had three emails from me, the last one inviting myself to visit. Clearly any right-minded person would have dismissed me as an over-keen stalker and simply blocked my email; instead, she replied with a cautious yes.

Once again, my communications skills had come in handy. I first visited Sydney in January 2000. Then I visited again. Then she visited me. Then I moved to Sydney. Then she moved to London. Then we got married. And so it was that, after four years of politics in London, I found myself flying to Sydney to start my career all over again in late 2005.

In 2006, I made the jump from politics and government into the world of creative brand strategy, joining the Australian arm of Jack Morton, at the time, the world's largest events company, based in the USA. The year before, in 2005, The Facebook had dropped its 'The' and began the evolution into Meta. That same year saw the launch of YouTube. Not long after, in 2007, Apple launched the iPhone and Brian Chesky launched Airbnb. In 2008, Spotify was born; then, in 2009, Uber; and in 2010, Instagram. Meanwhile, in 2008, Google released the first commercial version of Android, and in 2010, Samsung had the first true Android competitor to the iPhone, the Galaxy S.

Over that transformative five-year period from 2005 to 2010, the shared, social economy and the mobile economies were born. The intersection of those three economies gave birth to a fourth: the experience economy. At that stage, we were all still digital immigrants seeking to make sense of this fast-evolving world of new possibilities and new rules. Today, digital immigrants, like me, are trying to balance the knowledge and insights we bring from the 'before' times with the needs and expectations of generations of digital natives.

It was all of these experiences that shaped my instincts, my judgement and my beliefs in the power of narrative; in the building of brands as communities (or 'tribes' as Seth Godin would put it); in the importance of experiences; in the impact of word of mouth; in the transformative shifts in culture and marketing being driven by the rise of smartphones and social media; in the rise of purposeful, authentic brand-building; in the possibilities of direct-to-consumer (DTC) thinking; in the primary of great product; in the role of design and aesthetics. I brought all of this to the task of shaping the brand context around Four Pillars.

But the simple fact is that none of this would have happened if an email reply from that tall Australian girl had not landed in my inbox one morning in 1999. And now, 15 years later, another overnight email was going to change everything again.

Holy shit!!! Check out the bottom of the email below—DOUBLE GOLD MEDAL team! Now get your PR skates on!!!!!

That was the email Stu and I received from Cameron at 7.44 am on Tuesday 25 March 2014. And it was, in many ways, the starting gun for the Four Pillars Gin that exists today.

It might seem strange to devote part of a book about so much that actually happened to what didn't happen, but this is one of the things I have spent the most time reflecting on over the past decade. I'll give you the facts, and let you reflect on what you would have done.

In 2013, according to the International Wine and Spirits Report, Hendrick's had roughly 60 per cent of the super-premium gin market in Australia. In other words, six out of every ten bottles of gin over $70 sold in Australia went to one brand (Hendrick's) that had one single product.

Hendrick's was part of gin's third wave, showing consumers that gin could be more than London Dry Gin, and combining a quirky, curious, unusual brand personality with a simple but compelling signature serve, suggesting garnishing a Hendrick's G&T with a slice of cucumber.

In sending off two bottles of Rare Dry Gin to the San Francisco World Spirits Competition, Cam really didn't know what to expect. Back then, there was just one category for gin (today there are multiple categories, from 'London Dry' to 'contemporary' to 'flavoured') and that one category was dominated by London Dry styles. Cam was half-expecting the judges to reject our gin for being too citrus-forward, too flavourful and too distinct from the classic juniper-dominant London Dry style. And he certainly didn't expect every judge in the competition to give it a gold medal.

That's what double gold meant: unanimous golds from every judge. Four Pillars Rare Dry Gin was one of only nine gins in the world that year to receive that accolade. And that brings us to our next sliding doors moment.

Now we had our hero gin (Rare Dry), our signature serve (a wedge of orange in a G&T) and our big accolade (a double gold medal from San Fran), surely it was time to double-down on marketing, sales and growth, chipping away at Hendrick's huge 60 per cent market share? But, had we done that, the next decade would have been very different.

Our purpose would have gone unfulfilled. After all, how can you say you've elevated the craft of distilling gin in Australia with just a single gin (no matter how good)? And how bored would we have got making the same gin for the next ten years? And how quickly would the DNA of our business shift from making to marketing? And how relatively easy would it have been for others to imitate our one hero gin and erode what distinctiveness we had? On every level, I'm convinced that, had the temptation been there to simply focus on growing Rare Dry Gin, the Four Pillars we know and love today would never have happened. Luckily, we chose to walk a different path.

In my mind, 2014 was the year that Four Pillars Gin truly started to take shape. It was in March of that year that we walked through the sliding door that took Four Pillars in a very different direction. Perhaps, in that alternate universe, Four Pillars set aside its innovation plans and became hyper-focused on our hero Rare Dry Gin product, and became a singular and single-minded producer of one gin. But, in the universe I'm typing in, Four Pillars was already focusing on our next gins, and Cameron was already on the lookout for a permanent home for our gin dreams.

DRINKS BREAK NO.2:
The Gin & Tonic

The first gin and tonic was really just tonic. Brits sent to India would deal with the risks of malaria by drinking tonic water, made with the quinine-rich bark of the cinchona tree (quinine being a powerful anti-malarial). The tonic was bitter and hard to drink, so a slug of gin and a bit of lime made it all the more palatable. The G&T was borne and it was medicinal too.

I started to fall back in love with the gin and tonic (after years of being sworn off G&Ts) when on holiday with one of my great mates and his family in 2013. Rupinder had been one of my two best men back in 2002, and he would go on to be a founding Ginvestor in Four Pillars. We met up on the island of Lombok near Bali and Rupinder had brought a litre bottle of Bombay Sapphire.

Every evening, after a day of swimming in the pool and dodging the epic heat and humidity, we would park the kids in front of a movie and make a round of G&Ts for the adults. The G&Ts were classically made: a big slug of gin in a tall glass, a long pour of Schweppes tonic and a slice of lemon. I distinctly remember how brilliantly refreshing the first couple of sips were — that pine needle sharpness of the gin and the quinine-y bittersweetness of the tonic. But, by the end of the glass, I'd had enough and didn't want to go back for a second.

Eight months later when tasting my first Four Pillars Rare Dry G&T, the experience was completely different. Cameron had created a gin that was still built on a canvas of juniper, but his use of lemon myrtle and fresh oranges, combined with the use of spice and heat from the Tassie pepper and star anise, had created a gin that was dangerously drinkable and moreish. Shifting to Fever-Tree Mediterranean Tonic (softer and less bitter than regular Indian tonic) also made a massive difference, as did garnishing the drink with a wedge of fresh orange to bring out the orange notes in gin. Suddenly, the G&T was transformed for me, and I've never looked back. The challenge became to remind myself how quickly two or three G&Ts could disappear on a hot Australian evening!

Since making that first Rare Dry Gin, the first question for any gin we make has been, 'How does it go in a G&T?' Here are four of my favourite combinations.

No.1: Perfect G&T

30–45 ml Rare Dry Gin
90–120 ml tonic
Orange
Ice

Start with the gin. Pour Rare Dry Gin into a glass. Add tonic (I favour Fever-Tree's Light Mediterranean Tonic). Stir a few times, then fill the glass with as much good ice (small, sad flaky shards of ice will melt far too quickly in your drink) as you can lay your hands on. Stir again and garnish with a wedge of fresh orange.

Ice done right

I learned from better bartenders than me to build all the liquid in a drink before adding ice. That way you can see exactly what you're doing and properly stir the drink before adding the ice. On tonic, there's no set rule on the ratio of gin to tonic, but I favour 1:3. Remember that more ice means a colder drink and less dilution, which is what we want: an ice-cold G&T, not a watery, flat G&T.

No.2: Bloody G&T

45 ml Bloody Shiraz Gin
90 ml tonic
Orange or lemon
Ice

Ever since Cam first came up with his brilliant idea to combine our Rare Dry Gin with fresh local Shiraz grapes, we've debated the best way to drink it. Unquestionably delicious just over ice with a slice of orange or lemon, it's also outstanding with any form of lemon mixer, from bitter lemon to lemon tonic to old-fashioned lemonade. But I always come back to a simple Bloody G&T.

Consider going 1:2 with your tonic to gin ratio (so 45 ml Bloody Shiraz Gin to 90 ml of tonic) because there's plenty of naturally occurring sugar already in the gin. Add lots of ice, as always, and garnish with a slice of either orange or lemon.

Simply delicious

We wrestled for ages with the perfect serve to go with Bloody Shiraz Gin. After all, it was a Four Pillars invention, a true original, and so many people enjoy it simply on ice with a slice of citrus (and it's hard to make a bad drink with it). But ultimately we ended up back where we started... it makes a bloody great Bloody G&T.

No.3: Gin & Soda (or Sonic)

30–45 ml Fresh Yuzu Gin
100 ml soda water
Lemon
Ice

Depending on how much of a sweet tooth you have, you might want to make your G&T into a gin and sonic, effectively using half soda water and half tonic as your mixer (trendy bartenders coined the idea of a 'sonic' years ago and now everyone seems to have jumped on the lower-sugar bandwagon). This way, you get to enjoy the same long, effervescent drink, but with less sugar. And if you want to eliminate the tonic completely, we came up with a gin that we reckon works beautifully in a gin and soda.

Combine 30–45 ml of Fresh Yuzu Gin with 100 ml of soda water (try to track down a yuzu soda if you want to double down on bright citrus flavours). Fill the glass with ice and garnish with a lemon wheel.

Yuzu askew

Cameron's aim with our gins has always been to make gins that are hugely flavourful and aromatic, but also very well balanced. In the case of Fresh Yuzu Gin, he deliberately created a gin that was a little imbalanced but super bright and citrus-forward (albeit balanced with the use of some sencha genmaicha tea in the distillation) so the gin would still shine even when mixed with soda.

No.4: Gin & Ginger

30 ml Navy Strength Gin
100 ml ginger beer
Lime
Ginger
Ice

My father was a big fan of the Moscow Mule (a 1941 classic that combines vodka and ginger beer in a copper tankard to keep the drink super cold), and I've always loved drinks mixed with ginger ale or ginger beer. It also happens that a bunch of our gins go terrifically with ginger mixers.

If you're feeling brave, try Four Pillars Navy Strength with ginger beer. It goes down far too easily, so just remember the gin you're starting with is almost 50 per cent stronger than the regular stuff! Start with just 30 ml of Navy Strength Gin and 100 ml of ginger beer. Ginger beer or ale is also our preferred mixer with our Australian Christmas Gin. In either case, top up with ice and garnish with a combination of a slice of fresh lime, a lime leaf and some fresh ginger. So good!

Navy strength on the go

At the time of writing we've made four standout ready-to-drink gin drinks in cans, matching the four drinks in this drinks break. The standout for me? Navy Strength Gin and ginger, no question. Grab a four pack for your next BBQ and you won't look back!

TEN

From gin to gins ... and 'Made From Gin'

That email from San Francisco really lit a fire under our business, and we needed to direct all our focus into making sure every person in the country knew that Australia now made one of the world's best gins. Rare Dry Gin was already ranged in Dan Murphy's, so our efforts were focused on driving the rate of sale there; supporting the first indie retailers, small bars and restaurants who had supported us from day one; and driving people to our website.

Over the coming months, our efforts meant that by 1 August 2014 Four Pillars Rare Dry Gin was already available in over 500 liquor stores across Australia. Add in over 150 small bars, over 100 restaurants and around 20 five-star hotels and resorts, and our Australia-wide footprint was already significant and our belief in the power of hand-to-hand combat (tastings, masterclasses, events), generosity and hospitality was paying dividends.

And yet, while our focus was theoretically all on scaling Rare Dry Gin, we were already spreading our focus across multiple other bets. In February 2014, we started supplying an unlabelled overproof gin to the Gin Palace in Melbourne (the iconic OG small bar and unofficial home of gin culture in Australia as well as the scene of our first launch event). At first, this gin was just a higher proof version of Rare Dry Gin, but Cameron wasn't happy, and it was only once he'd added in ginger, turmeric and fresh native finger limes that he settled on a recipe for this, our landmark Navy Strength Gin.

Being in the middle of the Yarra Valley's wine country, Cameron quickly started to collect old wine barrels, so another gin was ageing away down the back of the winery. This one was Rare Dry Gin in old French oak, ex-Chardonnay barrels. By August, both Four Pillars Navy Strength Gin (originally called Four Pillars Gunpowder Proof Gin) and Four Pillars Barrel Aged Gin had been released—and these gins weren't the only things that were going to distract us from single-mindedly focusing on Rare Dry Gin. Because now we were about to get into the food business.

Long before Four Pillars became focused on being the world's most sustainable gin producer (a journey we're still on, and a destination we will never reach), a commitment to treading lightly on the planet was already ingrained in our DNA. It came from two places.

First was the fourth pillar of our purpose: Taking care of the communities our craft depends on. Of all the communities that come to mind, first and foremost are our Healesville neighbours. And taking care of them means taking care of the food- and drink-growing paradise that is our Yarra Valley home. So, seeking to minimise our water and energy usage and our waste came naturally to us.

Second is our obsession (specifically, Cameron's obsession) with process that, for us, is what craft is all about: being obsessed with the core processes at the heart of what you do, and seeking to do them better. For Cameron, that means a hatred of throwing flavour away—specifically the hundreds of kilograms of delicious gin-steamed oranges he and Wilma were creating in addition to an amazing gin.

Every batch of roughly 450 bottles of gin would leave us with about eight kilograms of gin-steamed oranges. These delicious unwaxed, organic oranges had been sliced in half and steamed in gin vapours for about eight hours, but were otherwise perfectly intact. If you were lucky enough to be there as Cam was emptying the cooling botanical basket after a distillation, Cam would invite you to take a bite out of one—and they were delicious, not boozy (all the alcohol had evaporated) and full of botanical flavours.

Cameron was scratching his head for something to do with all this precious citrus, and continuing to take them home to make orange cakes wasn't going to do anything for his waistline. And then he had a brainwave that was only possible because of his instincts and his relationships.

Cam asked local preserve maker and all-round legend Caroline Gray if she could do something with them. And, a few weeks later, we had our answer: a gin-steamed orange marmalade as well as an alternative version made with a dash of Campari, which we called a Breakfast Negroni. The first jars were unlabelled and sent as a surprise and delight gift to supporters and special customers. But, within a year, we had a formal label on both products and we'd won a world marmalade award—Wallpaper* in London included it in their annual design awards. Cam would joke that we were fast becoming a marmalade maker with gin as a side project. Ironically, our reputation as specialist gin-makers had been enhanced by making something that wasn't gin!

One of the things I'm most proud of through the Four Pillars journey is the frequency with which we would pause and make sure that whatever craft-led, quality-led decision we had just made was framed optimally with an eye on the long term. This moment of marmalade-making was one of the first of these. We could easily have said, 'the signature ingredient in Rare Dry Gin is our use of whole fresh oranges and we hate throwing this delicious gin-steamed fruit away, so we make marmalade with it'. We did say that, of course, but we also said, 'this marmalade is the first in our series of Made From Gin products, where we seek to give all the by-products of our distilling a second life'.

We didn't know then that we would end up making a gin salt with the wonderful makers at Olsson's, using spent gin botanicals, or a Rare Dry Gin chocolate with Hunted & Gathered, using both spent botanicals and a handful of oranges. We didn't know that we would send spent botanicals to a friendly local pig farmer to supplement his feed and grow a batch of Gin Pigs, which we could then give to favourite chefs around Australia (don't ask about the time we tried to fly one to Singapore) so we could host wonderfully indulgent, bacchanalian Gin Pig Dinners. We didn't know that our mate Jack Holman at Stone &

Crow cheese in the Yarra Valley would start using some of our stillage (the water left over in the stills after distillation) to wash the rind of a gin cheese we could one day serve as a snack in our distillery door, or that our mates at Yarra Valley Caviar would one day make a Bloody Shiraz soaked roe, or that our neighbour Ricci from Ricci's Bikkies would use our botanicals to make delicious crackers to go with our gin cheese.

We didn't know that we would hire Matt Wilkinson, a legendary Melbourne chef, to help us develop our Made From Gin program and our food and restaurant partnerships, even though we, ourselves, had no restaurant and no kitchen to speak of at the time. And we didn't know that Caroline, our wonderful marmalade maker, would end up joining our team fulltime to run the kitchen (as well as public marmalade-making sessions) in our newly expanded Distillery in 2022. All that was in the future. But back then, in 2014, we had the foresight to name and storytell our vision for being the world's most creative gin-maker, only making gin—except for all the other things we made from gin!

Talking of vision, far-sightedness and ambition, all this innovation—multiple gins, barrels to age gin, making and selling marmalade—was going to need more room. And Cameron had found it in an old timber yard on Lilydale Road in Healesville, a location that also happened to be less than 200 metres from Cam's house.

To highlight how much 2014 was a blur, it was only in looking back that I realised that Cam told Stu and me about the space he'd found the day before that life-changing email from San Francisco. In typical Healesville style, Cam had spotted the real estate agent outside the old timber yard and had got straight onto him to see the place the next day, before it had even hit the market. The place was a bit of a wreck, but beneath the clutter, the bones were solid.

But all that was ahead of us. Remember, by the beginning of December 2014, we'd still only been on the market for 12 months, but it already felt like we'd lived through the first three eras of Four Pillars:

- We'd launched three gins and two Made From Gin marmalades, with another gin about to be released before the year was over.

- Our Rare Dry Gin had won that double gold medal at the San Francisco World Spirits Competition and followed it up with gold medals for both Rare Dry Gin and Navy Strength Gin at the Hong Kong International Wine and Spirits Competition.

- Our sales target had doubled for the first six months of 2014 (selling 14 000 bottles of gin against a target of 7000 bottles) and had exceeded that number by the end of October, selling another 14 500 bottles before summer had even begun.

- We'd put our homes on the line to purchase an old timber shed in Healesville and had managed to get the financing together to begin the process of redeveloping it as the home of Four Pillars.

- We'd put orders in with CARL for another two stills: a larger version of Wilma called Jude (named after Stu's mum) and a scaled-down experimental still called Eileen (named after my mum who, fittingly, doesn't drink).

- We'd balanced all this scale and ambition with a delightfully silly and fun gin pop-up at Kitchen By Mike in Sydney, cementing our relationships with some great mates and supporters in Sydney, while infuriating Cameron with Stu's and my total lack of stock control and discipline (I think we gave away half the stock we were supposed to be serving and selling).

All told, 2014 was only just the beginning. All that thinking was being crafted into reality and it was working and growing. The only thing to do now was double-down.

USEFUL BIT #7:
STRATEGIC STORYTELLING

You're a new, fast-growing, under-resourced business. You're time-poor and budget-poorer.

You're faced with a sea of opportunities, a to-do list longer than there are hours in the week, and a bunch of opinions from the sidelines about everything you're doing wrong or not doing.

The daily demands on you as a leader mean you can barely see more than a few days ahead, but meanwhile, you're trying to keep both your business strategy (the rational side of your business) and your brand strategy (the emotional side) on course.

How do you stay focused on the big picture?

My suggestion to you is that now is not the time for complicated strategy models. Instead, burn (metaphorically at least) your business/management/brand strategy books. Throw away your OGSM and OKR templates (who cares what the ridiculous consultant acronyms mean anyway) and your 'brand house' models, and challenge yourself instead to craft a simple story that works for you. Then tell that story (to your team, your investors, your partners and yourself) as much as humanly possible.

Start by writing a strategy story that covers your:

- purpose and craft (your *why* and your *how*)

- hero product story (from founder backstory to reasons to believe in the product)

- understanding of your core customer (who are they and why will they buy?)

- insights into the category and the opportunity

YOUR STRATEGY STORY

YOUR PURPOSE AND CRAFT

YOUR WHY	YOUR HOW

YOUR HERO PRODUCT STORY

WHY YOUR PRODUCT IS
BETTER/DIFFERENT/THE ONLY

YOUR CORE CUSTOMER

WHO ARE THEY?	WHY WILL THEY BUY?

YOUR CATEGORY INSIGHTS

WHAT'S THE OPPORTUNITY?

YOUR AMBITION & THEORY OF GROWTH

WHAT GIVES YOU THE RIGHT TO WIN?

YOUR PLAYBOOK TO BUILD EMOTION & BIAS

HOW WILL YOU BUILD THE
BRAND YOU NEED?

- theory of growth and ambition

- right to win and the contributions of everyone in the business

- playbook to build emotion and bias (i.e. brand value) into your business.

Start with trying to capture all that in around 750 words. That should take you five minutes to tell. Rehearse telling yourself this story lots—in the shower, as you walk to work etc. Develop a conversational fluency with your strategy.

Then boil it down to the 300-word (two-minute) version. This is short enough that you can tell this simple strategy story at the start of every major meeting (with your team, your investors, your partners).

Make your story part of the myth-making rituals of your business and your culture. Make your strategy part of your everyday conversations. Turning your strategy into a story allows your leaders to make the story their own. In this way, your whole business can take ownership of the strategy, starting to make better, more aligned decisions without everyone needing to swallow a whole PowerPoint deck.

ELEVEN

Experiments that worked

What is it that makes Four Pillars a craft gin distiller? And not just any craft distiller, but arguably the best craft gin producer on the planet?

It can't be size—we never wanted our craft to be defined by smallness, and by selling more gin than Hendrick's in Australia in 2021, we couldn't claim to be truly small anymore. And it could never have been about charming inconsistency—Four Pillars drinkers around the world rely on every bottle of our multi-award-winning Rare Dry Gin delivering the same trademark hit of citrus aromatics and spicy deliciousness every time. So, what is it?

Looking back at everything that happened in 2014, you can see the first elements of what makes Four Pillars unique taking shape. There's the absolute focus and specialisation in gin, and with that focus and specialisation came the passion and attention to exploring what gin could be. This resulted in three benchmark gins in the first 12 months: our signature Rare Dry Gin, our overproof Navy Strength Gin and our sippable Barrel Aged Gin. At the time, producing such a range of unique and highly awarded gins all within the space of a year was unheard of. In addition, we started to explore the possibilities of flavour sustainability through our Made From Gin program.

The following year saw a lot happen, with two new gins adding another key strand to our Four Pillars identity: radical gin-fuelled experimentation. For me, being a 'craft' business is an attitude. It's about a commitment to quality of product, above all. It's about a willingness to experiment in the name of craft, having fun as gin-makers, and allowing that to lead everything we do. And it's about remembering, in a customer-obsessed world, that what customers really value are brands and producers with purpose, integrity and an ambition to create things beyond the obvious, beyond what the customer knows to ask for.

Take our Bloody Shiraz Gin and our Australian Christmas Gin – two things literally no one ever asked for, but that we made anyway. And thank goodness we did, because they are awesome. Both were Four Pillars inventions, entirely inspired by Cam's genius and instincts, and both changed the trajectory of Four Pillars forever. More than anything else we make, those two gins have come to define what Four Pillars is all about.

Four Pillars spent two years living in the back of Rob Dolan's winery before moving to our home in Healesville, and so many things happened there that shaped our future DNA. One of those was the decision to open our doors to the public for the first time on World Gin Day in June 2014. Cam and a few mates from the Yarra Valley moved all the barrels out of the way and set up a small tasting area outside Wilma's cage. Elton and Ebony, both local legends from Healesville who would go on to become huge parts of our business, were there wearing Four Pillars aprons, and we planned to spend the day offering tastings of Rare Dry Gin, the unlabelled and as-yet-unreleased Navy Strength Gin, and the just-released Barrel Aged Gin. Cameron, meanwhile, would offer mini tours around his tiny cage, showing off Wilma and answering questions about gin, distilling, botanicals and his best 400-metre time.

Stu couldn't make it down to Healesville (he was busy juggling oranges and offering tastings at the fancy new Dan Murphy's store in Sydney's Double Bay), but he did manage to get onto Sydney's 2GB and a bunch of Melbourne radio stations to spruik our first-ever open day. The response was ridiculous, and we were run off our feet the entire day while cars backed up Rob's driveway and onto Wonga Road.

At the end of the day, we celebrated in true Four Pillars style: with a Bucket of Shots from the local liquor store. A year later we were back there to do it all again, the same energy, the same Bucket of Shots waiting for us, and even more people lined up out of the warehouse doors—but also with one important upgrade to the whole experience.

Cameron had committed an act of petty theft that would change the course of Four Pillars (and arguably Australian gin) history. He'd stolen about 200 kilograms of Rob's Shiraz fruit.

Way back when we were developing our first six-pack cases, we were trying to be clever and future proof. We didn't know our mates at the Gin Palace were going to inspire us to make a Navy Strength Gin, but we did know that we planned to start barrel ageing some. We also thought that making a sloe gin was what a lot of serious gin-makers did (Plymouth in the UK is a great example), so we added three tick boxes on the side of the case: one for Rare Dry Gin, one for Barrel Aged Gin and one for Sloe Gin.

The months ticked by and occasionally a customer would ask us when our sloe gin was going to be released. The truth was that we hadn't even started working on a sloe gin, and none of us were sure we wanted to. Cam and Stu felt that commercial sloe gins were too packed full of sugar (a thesis borne out by a quick bit of lab testing), but without adding sugar, the infusion of sloe berries just created something tart and rather unpalatable. More to the point, we didn't like or drink sloe gin ourselves and neither did the few people we spoke to. Add in the fact that sloes don't grow in Australia in any great quantity, and you had to wonder why we were even thinking about this.

In 2015, Cam was still managing Rob's winery operations three days a week (and running Four Pillars the other four days a week). Towards the end of the vintage, Rob had a parcel of Shiraz fruit (beautiful cool climate Yarra Shiraz) that he didn't have an immediate use for. So inspiration struck and (without telling us or Rob) Cameron took it. Telling himself he was saving Rob the hassle of figuring out what to do with the fruit, Cam tipped gin from Wilma straight over the top of the fresh fruit and stirred it daily for eight weeks.

The result was extraordinary. The grapes soaked up the gin and the high proof Rare Dry Gin ripped them apart. After a light pressing, the juice was still gin, but gin that had taken a holiday in a grape and emerged full of purple colour and natural sweetness. Cam brought two bottles of his Shiraz gin experiment to our May 2015 Ginvestor meeting for everyone to taste. Everyone loved it, of course, and the rest was history.

But, still there were decisions to make. There was no time to get a label on this gin before World Gin Day, but did we really want to miss the chance of having a new gin to taste and talk about on what we had helped to make the biggest day on the gin calendar in Australia? No chance. So we quickly scrambled together 500 neck tags and came up with a name.

After much debating of names over email, Sally Lewis got the credit for naming our iconic invention. Fed up with the back and forth, she said to Stu, 'It's just bloody Shiraz gin, isn't it?' – and Bloody Shiraz Gin was born. We post-rationalised it with talk of the French rosé-making technique *saignée,* where colour is bled from the grapes, but in truth, it was a great example of backing a good idea and running with it.

A small, but critical, advantage on our side, as we continued to innovate and create new gins at speed, was how we leveraged the Four Pillars Gin name. Instead of looking to build very specific meaning into the name, with a locked-down definition of the Four Pillars, we instead treated the name as a philosophy, a belief in focusing on doing a few things well. Each gin we made had its own four pillars, described and celebrated on the side of the label.

In the case of Bloody Shiraz Gin, the four pillars were:

- No.1 YARRA. Our home is Healesville in the Yarra Valley. While we craft gin, our neighbours make some of the world's most terrific wines.

- No.2 SHIRAZ. Every vintage, we source the best Victorian Shiraz grapes we can get our hands on.

- No.3 SAIGNÉE. The French call one of the processes of giving rosé wine its colour 'saignée' meaning 'bleeding'.

- No.4 SWEET. Shiraz grapes are steeped in gin for eight weeks before being pressed to release the ginny juice full of colour, flavour and delicious natural sweetness. We recommend, where possible, you drink it young and fresh with a splash of tonic and a squeeze of fresh lemon.

Now, for the first time, we weren't just making traditional-style dry and barrel-aged gins in a modern Australian style, we were making a completely different and new gin. To our knowledge, no one in the world had developed a fresh Shiraz-based grape gin like this (plenty had distilled using a grape-based spirit, but no one was steeping all the colour, flavour and sweetness of fresh grapes into their gin). This was truly taking advantage of our place in Australia and in Victoria's Yarra Valley to make utterly unique gin. And the response was phenomenal.

Gin fans who tasted it on World Gin Day couldn't believe how delicious it was, and Cameron's 500 bottles disappeared within days. By September, we were already thinking about how much fruit we would need to secure the following vintage to make ten times the quantity. But, by the time we got to the beginning of June 2016, on what we christened Bloody Shiraz Day, it was clear that we'd undercooked things again. Those 5000 bottles were gone in 48 hours.

For four years we played cat and mouse with Shiraz quantities, never wanting to lose the vintage specialness of what we had created, but equally wishing it would last just a little bit longer! Either way, this was what we had built our Batch No.1 community for: exclusive early access to limited-edition gins. And thanks to the growth of our brand combined with the deliciousness of this gin, Bloody Shiraz Gin always felt too limited, no matter how much we made!

In 2023, Four Pillars was crushing more Shiraz fruit than any wine producer in the Yarra Valley. But, once again, I'm getting ahead of myself, because there was one more gin to create yet. Another gin that would spark an annual tradition and give Four Pillars a place in the hearts of thousands of gin lovers.

Australian Christmas Gin began as an experiment by Cameron who wanted to see what would happen if he distilled Christmas puddings. It was his way of honouring his mum's tradition of making puddings every Derby Day weekend (she always used the recipe from the 1968 *Woman's Weekly* guide to Christmas cooking). The experiment continued when he stumbled upon some 100-year-old Muscat barrels that struck him as perfect for ageing a Christmassy gin. At no stage did he (or we) stop to ask: who would buy this? That wasn't relevant. What was relevant was a much more basic set of questions. First, should

Four Pillars make this? And, second, will it be awesome? In other words, as long as it excited Cameron and Stuart, it would be worth making. Whether anyone would buy it was never a consideration worth slowing down for. Our commitment to our craft demanded that the product be made.

The first batch of Australian Christmas Gin was made using some extra puddings Cam got his daughters to make in 2015. His mum Wilma had always dragged Cam and his four brothers into the kitchen every year to make puddings, and Cam wanted to torture his three girls with the same family tradition. It was while reading through his mum's 1968 recipe (he still has it, complete with Wilma's handwritten annotations) that he got the idea to distil the puddings. The girls were tasked with making some extra, and Cam went and distilled them alongside our signature botanicals that afternoon.

The resulting gin was Christmassy, but not rich or indulgent enough for Cameron. Luckily, the answer came in the form of the two old Muscat barrels. Originally from William Grant in Scotland, these barrels (we called them Statler and Waldorf after the old boys in the Muppets) had been ageing Muscat in Rutherglen for about 80 years. Muscat screamed Christmas to Cameron, so he decided to age his new pudding gin experiment in the barrels. And, later, he decided to add a splash of fresh Muscat to the final gin before bottling. The core recipe for Australian Christmas Gin was in place.

When it came to bottling our first batch of Australian Christmas Gin, I wanted the label to do justice to why it existed: as a celebration of Christmas and of creativity in our craft. I decided the label should feature an artwork and no dominant branding. The logic was sound, but also scary. The thought process was that this gin stemmed from Cameron's family tradition and we wanted it to become part of other people's Christmas family traditions. We wanted people to be able to gift and enjoy it at Christmas. We wanted it to look like a present and a work of art. We wanted to solve the problem of gift-wrapping it by wrapping it in a beautiful label. And we wanted to be able to celebrate each individual year so that people could build a tradition of collecting the bottles, each with their own unique artwork. It's a source of great pride to me that we had the foresight to execute this strategy in 2016, laying the groundwork for years of artwork and releases to come.

The only question was, how would people respond to this odd gin with the branding-free art label? In short, they loved it, and we ran out far too quickly, despite the concerns of one retailer who asked me, 'How will people know what it is?' (Two days later that same retailer had sold out and was asking our distributor for another case.)

The copy on the side of the label describes Australian Christmas Gin as a tribute to four things Cameron loves: Australia, Christmas, gin and his late mum Wilma. It was, and remains, all of those things, but to me it is also, in its origin story, in its commitment to experimentation, and in its rejection of commercial considerations, a perfect tribute to what we've always tried to do as a craft-led business.

Over the first eight releases of Australian Christmas Gin, we've sold a lot of gin, and we've made a lot of Christmas Days pretty joyous. I know that from the hundreds of emails and social media messages we've received from people around Australia and around the world sharing their Australian Christmas Gin stories with us. It tastes of Australia; it tastes of Christmas; and it tastes of tradition, nostalgia and family.

Above all, Australian Christmas Gin has never been about the sales for us; it's always been about the craft, the story, the labour of love, and the reminder that we should begin every day with a desire to do new, interesting and sometimes random things in the name of gin and gin-making.

Christmas Gin also inspired us to create the Four Pillars Christmas (Gin) Revue, a raucous annual tradition of storytelling, singing, drinking and feasting led by Stu and Cam, which has been steadily professionalised over the years. I genuinely believe no other spirits business on the planet could have pulled off both the quality and seriousness of the gins we were making and the absolutely irresponsible silliness of our Christmas revues all at once (as survivors of many revues will doubtless testify).

Our Christmas revue events were just one example of how we matched the uniqueness and creativity of our gin-making with a unique approach to how we shared the craft of our gin.

USEFUL BIT #8:
A FOUR PILLARS EXAMPLE

At Four Pillars, our purpose has never changed. But, over time, we've become clearer on how we want that purpose to be felt by our customers.

When we put together our first official, grown-up brand playbook (allowing the brand's guidelines to be understood by everyone and not just live in our heads), we captured the four ways we wanted people to feel when they came into contact with Four Pillars. We also identified which touchpoints were most essential to delivering each feeling.

The bottom line was that we wanted people to feel the love and attention to detail that goes into every bottle of gin (we still do, because the love is stronger than ever!). If we could, we would force every customer to watch us make a batch of gin. But we can't. So instead, we need to ensure that our commitment to craft, to quality, to creativity, to flavour, to attention to detail shows us in everything we do—from our labels to our photography to our storytelling to the packaging you receive your website orders in.

We also want people to feel they're doing business with a distillery in the Yarra Valley (because they are), so we try to make sure that every social media and email interaction creates a connection between our customers and our home. We want to feel small. We want to feel generous. We want people to feel that we take our gin seriously, but we don't take ourselves too seriously. There's a lot of stuff we want them to feel! We spend a lot of time talking about that, reviewing our tone in social media posts and email responses, and always checking in to make sure we've never gone too far with photography, content or a campaign. Our feelings benchmarks give us those guardrails.

OUR TIMELESS PURPOSE

* ELEVATE THE CRAFT OF GIN DISTILLING IN AUSTRALIA

* CELEBRATE THE CRAFT OF COCKTAILS IN AUSTRALIA

* SHARE THE CRAFT OF MODERN AUSTRALIA

* SUPPORTING THE COMMUNITY THAT MAKES OUR CRAFT POSSIBLE

OUR FEELINGS BENCHMARKS

FOUR PILLARS GIN IS THE MOST...

- CREATIVE (PRODUCTS & PARTNERSHIPS)

- DELICIOUS (DRINKS & CONTENT)

- WELL-DESIGNED (PHYSICALITY & GRAPHICS)

- GREAT FUN (EXPERIENCES & SOCIALS)

... BRAND IN GIN.

OUR STRATEGY STORY (2015)

FOUR PILLARS CRAFT

ELEVATE THE CRAFT
OF GIN DISTILLING

CREATE NEW POSSIBILITIES
FOR THE CRAFT OF GIN

CELEBRATE THE CRAFT OF
THE COCKTAIL

SHARE THE CRAFT OF
MODERN AUSTRALIA

FOUR PILLARS PLAYBOOK

DISTILLERY:
BUILDING THE WORLD'S LEADING
GIN DESTINATION

DIGITAL:
BUILDING DEEP, DIRECT, INTIMATE
RELATIONSHIPS WITH CONSUMERS,
TRADE AND INFLUENCERS

DISTRIBUTION:
BUILDING POWERFUL
PARTNERSHIPS WITH IMPORTERS,
DISTRIBUTORS, RETAILERS AND
BUSINESSES AROUND THE WORLD

DISRUPTION:
CONTINUING TO INNOVATE, PARTNER
AND CO-CREATE, APPLYING OUR
CRAFT AND CREATIVITY TO
CHALLENGE THE STATUS QUO

FOUR PILLARS FOCUS

CRAFT GIN DEPTH, COLLABORATION, EXPLORATION AND ENGAGEMENT

DIGITAL ENGAGEMENT, INNOVATION AND CUSTOMER INTIMACY

BARTENDER AND TRADE ENGAGEMENT, EDUCATION AND COLLABORATION

TOURISM AND EXPERIENCE INNOVATION AND THE CREATION OF AUSTRALIA'S HOME OF CRAFT GIN

GIFTING, PACKAGING AND RETAIL INNOVATION

CREATIVE PARTNERSHIP AND AUSTRALIAN/MELBOURNE/YARRA CRAFT AMBASSADORSHIP AND LEADERSHIP

SOCIAL IMPACT AND BUSINESS INNOVATION

On the strategy side, as we grew, we also developed different stories of where our focus would be. These stories were often written after the decisions were made: as a craft-led, maker business, we always backed our maker instincts. But even the retrospective act of sense-making those decisions (why are we doing the things we're doing?) helped the whole team understand our choices and our strategy.

Two extracts here (one from our 2015 strategy and one from our 2019 strategy) highlight the different approaches you can take. In 2015, we articulated the logic of our craft focus and our growth playbook to generate a list of all the key initiatives (the big bets) we were making.

In 2019, we captured our opportunity and the big idea behind what we were trying to do. And we used that to put all our activity into four big categories of focus.

There's no right way to tell or structure these stories. Do whatever works for you, for your style and for your business. Hopefully, what you can see in these Four Pillars examples is the consistency of the story, the thinking and the focus over time. That, far more than the structure of your strategy, is what I think matters most.

OUR STRATEGY STORY (2019)

FOUR PILLARS GIN IS A MODERN AUSTRALIAN MAKER OF THE WORLD'S BEST CRAFT GIN. AND THAT MATTERS FOR TWO REASONS:
1. NOWHERE TASTES LIKE AUSTRALIA
2. NOWHERE COMBINES SERIOUS QUALITY WITH THE REJECTION OF OVER-SERIOUSNESS LIKE AUSTRALIA

COMBINE MAKING THE MOST SERIOUS (AND SERIOUSLY DELICIOUS) RANGE OF GINS ON THE PLANET WITH MAKING LOTS OF BEAUTIFUL, DESIGNFUL, COLOURFUL, AND, YES, SERIOUSLY FUN THINGS TO DRIVE CUSTOMER INTIMACY WITH OUR CRAFT AND INVITE PEOPLE AROUND THE WORLD TO BE PART OF OUR (BETTER) GIN DRINKING AND LOVING COMMUNITY.

MAKING GIN
(AND MADE FROM GIN)

EXPERIENCES AND PARTNERSHIPS
(MARKETING THROUGH MAKING)

CONTENT AND ENGAGEMENT
(STORYTELLING TO MATCH THE STORYDOING)

BETTER GIN DRINKING COMMUNITY
(THE WORLD'S MOST ENGAGED CLUB OF GIN LOVERS)

PART THREE

Sharing

TWELVE

Launch as you mean to go on

Decisions are the thread that runs through this book. Okay, decisions and gin are the twin threads that run through this book. And once we'd made that big decision to lead with a modern Australian style of gin, giving Cameron the opportunity to get busy experimenting with Wilma in what would become Rare Dry Gin, and before we faced those sliding doors moments of 2014 when we decided to stay the course on exploring gins of many styles, we had a decision to make that wasn't gin-led (but which did create the foundations for all the gin-making to come). The decision was about how to launch this gin brand of ours to the world.

There were two dimensions to the decision about how to launch: timing and tradition.

The timing question was one of liquid: how could we launch Four Pillars without at least some level of liquid development? From conversations with potential investors to conversations with major retailers, how much was there to say without some gin samples to show off? Surely, if our major story was about the flavour advantages of Australia and turning those advantages into a gin, people needed to be able to taste it?

The tradition question was even more challenging. Traditional wisdom had it that you built your spirits brand on-premise (i.e. in great bars) and scaled and monetised it in the off-premise (i.e. liquor stores). This thinking (while clearly true for the most part) had three significant flaws. Understanding these three challenges and finding ways to address them, while still playing the traditional spirits game, was key to shaping the long-term DNA of the Four Pillars business.

The first challenge was a financial one. The received wisdom was that it was hard to make money in spirits in Australia because of the punitive levels of excise we pay in this country. To place this in perspective, Australia is the third-highest taxed country in the world when it comes to spirits, and spirits producers pay far more in excise than our friends over in the wine industry. In February 2024, the excise rate for spirits increased to $101.85 per pure litre of alcohol, which came on the back of regular increases (once or often twice every year) since the creation of Four Pillars in 2013. This means that roughly the first $30 of a $75 bottle of Rare Dry Gin goes straight to excise, making it hard for the producer to make any money while also paying distribution and retailer margins. The implication for a new, small (but ambitious) brand like Four Pillars was that depending on third-party distributed sales alone would simply not be a viable platform to grow a brand to scale.

The second challenge was a brand one. Stu, Cam and I had all worked in and consulted to wine brands and had seen the challenges they faced when it came to telling their brand story to their drinkers. Beyond creating a great cellar door experience for visitors to their regions, Australian wine producers (with one or two notable exceptions, like Penfolds) were struggling to project their brands to a wider audience of drinkers. Our realisation was that relying on our presence in bars, restaurants and retail stores to tell our brand story wouldn't be enough. We really needed to find a way to build direct relationships with our drinkers.

The third challenge was a future-ready one. In 2013, we were just beginning to see the disruptive power of social media in business, but the alcohol industry seemed to be almost completely unaffected. It simply didn't make sense to build a spirits business in 2013 and not build it social-first. And, yet, it wasn't clear how we could align a social-first approach (with all its implications and possibilities for building a direct relationship with end consumers) with a commercial model that traditionally focused on selling and storytelling through third parties.

As we thought about this more, it became clear that we were wrestling with two questions here: not just how we were going to launch, but how our launch would set the tone for our growth over the long term. Our answer to this critical question was really shaped by Stu and my wife Rebecca. Between them, they would champion a two-pronged approach to navigating the competing tensions and priorities of our launch: Stu, with his passion for relationships and influence; and Rebecca, with her curiosity about the emerging possibilities of the social media landscape and ability to get intimate and direct with our future drinkers and fans.

For Stu, all business is about relationships. And lucky for me and Cam, Stu brought that same relationship obsession to Four Pillars. Stu had spent the past 15 years building a PR agency, Liquid Ideas, with his wife Sally, so not only did he know everyone in booze (and beyond), but he understood how to earn media coverage, and he would keep us relentlessly focused on maintaining the quality of our relationships in the media and drinks trade.

Had Stu and Cam been the only voices in this conversation, I suspect we would have leaned a little more towards the more traditional path to launching and growth (focused on the trade and media first and foremost) and we would have done it brilliantly. In fact, fast-forward to December 2013, and that's exactly what we did. But thanks to the presence of Rebecca, by December we already had huge momentum in the business. And that was down to the non-traditional strand to our launch. It was the combination of the two approaches that ultimately shaped the Four Pillars approach to growth.

Bec's professional background is in the arts, where she'd worked in marketing and partnership roles for the likes of the Imperial War Museum, Churchill Museum and Cabinet War Rooms and the National Theatre in London, the Madison Square Park Conservancy in New York City, and the Sydney Festival, Sydney Youth Orchestras and De Quincey Co in Sydney. Her artsy resumé is relevant because it serves to illustrate a point: that the right strategy is both the one that will work *and* the one you (and the people around you) are best placed to execute. It also explains why, more than any of the three of us (white, male, middle-aged) co-founders, she could see the potential to build a brand that combined the best of both worlds: great drinks trade and media relationships, and intimate relationships with end consumers. She was simply much closer to and fluent with the disruptive forces blowing through the media and creative arts landscape.

Rebecca started to get seriously involved with Four Pillars in the middle of 2013. With about six months to go before our December launch, Stu, Cam and I needed a partner to execute everything that was outside of Cam's gin-making remit. With Cam assembling Wilma and figuring out everything from sourcing botanicals to sourcing bottles, someone needed to lead the charge on our brand development, label design, photography, content, collateral, website, social media footprint and launch events. That person was Bec (with help from my small brand consultancy and Stu and Sally's exceptional PR efforts).

By borrowing Bec from her career in the arts, we brought an arts marketing mindset into our business from the outset. This reinforced our 'makers, not marketers' DNA, ensuring that marketing was also seen as being in service of the making, and that the tail would never wag the dog.

The thing about arts marketing is that it only works in the long run if the art is compelling. Clever marketing can, perhaps, sell out the first few shows but, beyond that, reviews and word of mouth will be key. The task of an arts marketer is to creatively curate truths, not invent fictions. That philosophy matched perfectly with our ambitions for Four Pillars and our belief in the primacy of earned media over paid media.

In short, our job was to make genuinely good, compelling, delicious gins, and then make sure people heard about it. And by committing to being a craft business that placed process and quality above everything else, we had the ingredients to tell a story grounded in truth, not fiction.

This PR-led approach in itself would have been a differentiator in a spirits industry driven mostly by advertising and big global brands (think Smirnoff, Absolut, Gordon's, Jack Daniel's). But, while working through the launch strategy with Rebecca, it became clear that we had a chance to be even more disruptive.

If PR was too often an afterthought for the big booze brands, DTC (direct-to-consumer marketing and selling) was a complete blind spot. I had long been fascinated by Aesop and its focus on leading with its own bricks-and-mortar retail stores to drive its brand. But, then in the early 2010s, a whole new species of online-first DTC brands arrived to disrupt whole categories. Warby Parker (eyewear) was founded in the USA in 2010, swiftly followed by both Bailey Nelson and Oscar Wylie in Australia in 2012. Caspar (mattresses and bedding) was founded in the USA in 2014, again quickly followed by Ecosa, Koala and Sleeping Duck here in Australia. Then there was Frank Green (reusable water bottles) founded in Melbourne in 2014, and Zoë Foster Blake's Go-To Skincare, also founded in 2014.

Some of these brands retailed exclusively online using their own websites. Others operated a hybrid retail model of some direct sales and some retail partners. But the common DNA was an absolute focus on building a direct, intimate relationship between the brand and the consumer. This was something that the spirits industry was missing (in contrast to the craft beer movement, where craft brewers were deeply and directly engaged with their drinkers).

I wanted to understand why this was the case in spirits, and the answer seemed to come down to two things. First, 99 per cent of spirits retail happened through bricks-and-mortar bottle shops, so most brands were focused on traditional approaches ('above the line' advertising and 'below the line' trade marketing). Second, most of the big spirits brands were owned by global players (the likes of Bacardi, Beam Suntory, Diageo, Pernod Ricard and William Grant & Sons) who simply didn't have the appetite to build brand and community in a market the size of Australia.

Just as we had decided to make modern Australian gin, and reject the well-trodden path of starting with London Dry Gin, surely we could also take the marketing road less travelled, and create a strategy that began with DTC? Not only would it help us build more powerful connections with influential, early-adopting consumers, but, I reasoned, those consumers would go on to influence many more to purchase through traditional channels (bottle shops and bars).

Meanwhile, Bec was fascinated by the role that crowdfunding and social media was starting to play in the arts space, and it was thanks to her passion and expertise that we made Four Pillars the world's first gin brand to be launched via a crowdfunding platform (we launched our campaign on Pozible in October 2013, just two months after Mr Black, another Australian spirits success story, launched theirs on Kickstarter).

Ultimately, we decided to launch through crowdfunding because we were aligned on the importance of customer intimacy and direct sales for the future growth of our business. The Pozible campaign, as we saw it, would help build some initial momentum around this direct community. What we didn't know was what an impact it would have on our commitment to storytelling and customer intimacy, and on the role of direct releases to drive our brand and our bottom line.

There's something fascinating that happens when you're required to sell gin (or any tangible, sensory, taste-based product) without being able to showcase the product. It forces you to sell something more than just the functional benefits (e.g. the flavour) and focus instead on the story, the purpose, the ambition and the values behind the product. In other words, we had to sell the idea of Four Pillars before Cameron had finalised the gin (he had, at least, narrowed down the list of hero botanicals we'd be using so we didn't sound completely naïve).

Across the campaign we built for Pozible, we talked at length about our ambitions, about the journey we'd been on to research gin and about the vision we had for gin in Australia. And we also talked on a human scale about who we were, about how personal this was for us, and how we invited everyone who joined our campaign to come along with us on the journey and be part of making something special happen.

In that way, our approach to storytelling helped drive our commitment to intimacy. We got people involved and we made it clear we wanted to keep them involved. So, while our campaign included playful imagery of Wilma and our bottle and label prototypes, it also included real, raw footage of Cam collaborating with CARL's master distiller, Dr Klaus Hagman, who had come out to Australia to help Cam get the best out of Wilma (in between frequent jetlag-induced naps).

It was this combination of beauty (showcasing the craft and attention to detail at the heart of our gin business) and reality (revealing the hard work and human effort behind everything we made) that would go on to set the tone for our storytelling for years to come. This, for us, was craft intimacy in action. I reminded everyone about getting the balance right in an email on 27 October 2013, just before the Pozible campaign went live:

> *Remember we're craft ... so it's big love and attention to detail, not big money, that's driving Four Pillars. So, no big brand marketing bullshit or hubris. That said, we also want to be the best craft brand in Australia, so let's behave that way from day one ... this is definitely a passion project, but it is not a hobby or plaything!*

It was this combination of storytelling and intimacy that enabled the final piece of the jigsaw: community. When we submitted our draft campaign to the Pozible team for review before our launch, we received mostly positive feedback, but with a warning. The warning was that our cheapest 'reward' was too expensive. We had taken the view that the minimum Pozible pledge should be to purchase a single bottle of Batch Number One Rare Dry Gin for $70. Pozible's expert opinion was that successful campaigns needed to have a more accessible reward at the $10 to $20 mark, like a baseball cap or a T-shirt.

We stuck to our guns because, as a craft-led gin-maker, we didn't want to sell anything that didn't begin with a bottle of gin. We also didn't believe you would really be a member of our community until you'd tasted our Rare Dry Gin, so that had to be the minimum point of entry. Each of these first-batch bottles would be individually numbered and hand-signed by Cam.

The interesting add-on was to bundle in membership to our Batch No 1 Club with each first-batch bottle. This meant you would get VIP early access to every future first-batch release in perpetuity. Looking back, this commitment set us on a path of valuing our database and our early access subscribers who would grow us into being a limited-edition, gin-releasing juggernaut over the coming years, allowing us to build our brand and our bottom line at the same time. And it was all thanks to a decision to have a crack at running a crowdfunding campaign while we waited for Cam to finalise the gin recipe. Was it luck, judgement or a bit of both?

Either way, Rebecca nailed the execution (just as Cam and Stu would go on to nail the gin and the 'traditional' launch events a few weeks later) and we had now hardwired the importance of both crafted, long-form storytelling and intimate, loyalty-driving community engagement into our business. Our brand was set up to grow at the speed of social (by which I mean communicating in real time with a direct consumer audience, and not reliant on the traditional slow rhythms of advertising campaigns), doing justice to all the gin releases, innovations and partnerships that lay ahead of us. We had a direct line to our drinkers (albeit starting with a very small community of them) and we had hardwired the value of these intimate relationships into our business, seeing firsthand how it could positively impact our discussions with investors and partners (our Pozible success helped us close our Ginvestor conversations in a week, while we confidently told the team at Dan Murphy's that our DTC commitment would benefit their sales as much as ours).

What we didn't know, yet, was the extent to which our focus on intimacy was about to unleash another wave of innovation onto our little gin business.

USEFUL BIT #9:
CONVERSATION HIERARCHY

I've been incredibly fortunate with the influences and informal mentors I've learned (and stolen) from over my career. One of the most consistent themes has been to celebrate the importance of language and storytelling, both in the form of compelling, punchy messaging, and rich, in-depth narrative. It doesn't matter whether you're in politics, business, the charity sector, sport or the arts, the same question comes up again and again:

What's your story?

Whether you're building a fast-moving, consumer-facing, social-first DTC brand or a dry, complex, highly technical B2B (business-to-business) company—when it comes to growing your business, little (aside from the core craft or expertise that your product is based on) matters more than your storytelling.

In Useful Bit #7, I focused on how to develop your strategy through the lens of storytelling (shaping the stories you need to tell yourself and your colleagues as you navigate all the decisions you need to make). In this Useful Bit the focus is on your external story. The things you want the people who matter to you (your customers, your shoppers, your users, your stakeholders) to know about you. There are a number of things at play here, anchored in your conversation hierarchy. Let's work through them one by one.

Conversation hierarchy

This tool, introduced to me by my long-term strategy partner Amber Groves, helps you build out both the breadth and depth of the story you want to tell. You can apply it to your overarching business, to a new product you're releasing or

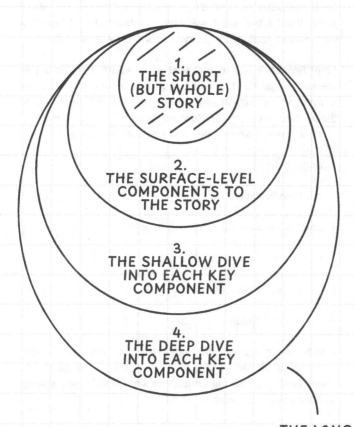

1.
THE SHORT
(BUT WHOLE)
STORY

2.
THE SURFACE-LEVEL
COMPONENTS TO
THE STORY

3.
THE SHALLOW DIVE
INTO EACH KEY
COMPONENT

4.
THE DEEP DIVE
INTO EACH KEY
COMPONENT

THE LONG
STORY

even to a particular audience you are targeting (e.g. CIOs and IT decision-makers for a B2B software company).

Approach it by thinking of your business story (the conversation you'd ideally like to have) at different levels:

Level one asks you to define the short version of the whole story. What's the most succinct, crystallised and powerful way you can capture the story of your business or product?

Level two asks you to pull that story apart, but remain at the surface level. How could you make sense of your story in three to five high-level messages or points? What should those messages cover? How would your ideal conversation unfold? Things I would value and consider include your:

• origin story

• purpose/ambition

• point of view on the world/key insight

• offering/hero product

• craft/hero capability

• difference/reason to choose.

If level one gives you your elevator pitch, level two is what you'd tell a customer CEO at a quick meet and greet. It's about capturing the full breadth of what makes you special without going into depth or detail.

At Four Pillars, our level one is about being modern Australian gin-makers, making gins we could only make here in Australia. Then level two would unpack our focus on flavour and drinkability, experimentation and creativity, hospitality and community, and our place and sustainability.

Level three, then, is about taking a shallow dive into each of the main areas of your story. And *level four*, finally, gives you the deep dive.

This is a rough framework, of course, and four things and four levels may not be right for you, but the logic is solid. Can you tell your whole customer-facing story succinctly and conversationally? Can you quickly capture the full breadth of your higher purpose/ambition, the core of what your business or product does, the value you create for your customers/ users, and the differentiating ways you create that value? And can you deep dive into each area on a case-by-case basis, depending on audience, medium and objective?

This is the mastery of your story that your conversation hierarchy gives you. And from here, writing social media posts, LinkedIn articles, customer emails, investor decks and business plans all gets a lot easier.

Storytelling tone, style and personality

The second side to getting your storytelling right is to understand your tone, style and personality. Who do you want the reader to picture when they read or hear your story being told? What associations do you want them to make? What emotions do you want them to feel? The way you deliver your story needs to align with the brand emotions and feelings you defined on page 78, whether that storytelling shows up on the side of a gin label, on the side of a delivery truck or at the start of a sales meeting.

At Four Pillars, we were lucky to have an abundance of writing talent in house. Stu and I are both excellent writers (well, he's excellent and I'm fast). Stu has more natural flair, gusto and humour; I'm more nuanced, strategic and precise (AKA dull and dry). Between the two of us, we were able to set a direction and tone for the brand that a fast-growing team, led by Rebecca, was able to master and make their own. Let's look at some practical ways you can identify and set the tone, style and personality for your brand.

Messengers and personification

One way you can help to set the tone for your business is to identify your hero storytellers and start to think about them as the personification of your business.

At Four Pillars, we were fortunate to have three co-founders who are experienced speakers and storytellers, giving us multiple faces and voices for the brand and the ability to match different founders to different audiences and environments.

Ultimately, it was Cameron, with his dedication and seriousness around the craft of distilling, but also his brilliant sense of humour, his naturally self-deprecating personality and his love of hospitality and meeting people, who helped the wider team nail the tone of Four Pillars. Too much 'Matt' in our tone of voice and we could sound over-serious; too much 'Stu' and we could sound too frivolous. Just the right amount of Matt and Stu, but with a big dose of Cam, and we were on safe ground!

Who gives your business a face and a voice? And who can you use as a reference point for the personification of your brand?

Audiences, touchpoints and channels

Who are you trying to talk to? Are you clear on your different audiences, customers and stakeholders and what will influence them? Feel free to carve up your conversation hierarchy this way too.

And where does your story need to show up? Which touchpoints matter most? Which communications channels have the potential for the greatest positive impact on your business and your growth? For example, every time Four Pillars released a new gin, Stu would take the lead on crafting a press release full of technical gin information combined with colourful storytelling. This, combined with our commitment to stunning editorial images of every gin we made, helped us secure the coverage we hoped for.

THIRTEEN

Collaborative to the core

As much as I have talked about our launch through crowdfunding being a rejection of the traditional approach to launching a spirits brand, the reality is that we also valued the more traditional relationships with the trade and drinks media immensely. Even before we had moved into a permanent brand home, with Cam and Wilma stuck in that small cage at the back of Rob's winery, we valued and took every opportunity to host trade and industry friends.

One of the best decisions we made early on in our journey was to engage James France and his Vanguard team to be our distributors. Vanguard wasn't the biggest player by a long way, but when it came to high-end influential bars and bartenders, it was by far the most respected. James had made his name by bringing the best and most interesting spirits into Australia, free from the constraints of the big global drinks companies.

So, if you were a bartender and wanted to get hold of Fortaleza tequila, Flor de Caña rum or any number of interesting mescals, vermouths, bitters, syrups and liqueurs, James was your guy. What James didn't have was a blockbuster gin brand or a strong relationship with consumer retail (his business was heavily bar focused). But that was perfect for us—we would bring the gin, the consumer brand-building and the retail focus, and James's team could focus on helping us build credibility and listings in Australia's best bars.

As soon as we'd launched Rare Dry Gin, the opportunities to host and engage bartenders came thick and fast. Stu emphasised the need to build and deepen our relationships with the on-trade (bars and restaurants), and the Vanguard team leveraged their greatest asset beyond the gin itself: the proximity of our Distillery and distiller. It might seem like a small and obvious thing looking back, but the reality in 2014 was that few bartenders or sprits retailers had ever experienced world-class gin-making close up.

Our belief in growing our business through hand-to-hand combat (visiting and engaging every bartender we could and, in return, inviting them to visit us) meant Cam had a steady stream of interesting bartenders walking through those Warrandyte doors. In hosting these talented drinks makers, it became clear that, while Cam was doing a phenomenal job of turning Australia's botanicals and fresh produce into a world-class drink, these folks knew far more than us about great drinks.

One of our earliest examples of this was a conversation with the team at The Rook. Sadly, no longer with us, The Rook was a dedicated gin bar in Sydney's CBD. The Rook's head bartender was Cristiano Beretta, a talented Italian with a passion for great drinks. He and his boss, Jason Williams, both had strong views on the Negroni, and what would make the perfect Negroni gin. Our view was that Rare Dry Gin already had what it took to be great in a Negroni (those big fresh orange notes played perfectly with the Campari and the vermouth), but Jason and Cristiano felt we could do even better.

On the back of these conversations, we invited Jason to come down to make gin with Cam, and explore what the ultimate Negroni gin would involve. The result, thanks to Jason's guidance and Cam's genius, was a super spicy gin that used Indonesian cubeb, African grains of paradise and whole fresh blood oranges. Cam was also able to get Wilma to showcase her versatility, tweaking the dials to make a funky, less pure gin that would stand up to the dominant, bittersweet flavours of the Campari and the sweet vermouth.

We called it Spiced Negroni Gin, with a clear preference for three-name gins starting to creep into our brand language. As with so many things in life, rules and guardrails enable not inhibit creativity, so giving ourselves a framework to naming every gin became very helpful. Critically, this gin marked the first time we had officially collaborated with a bartender to make a gin, so we called it the first of our new Bartender Series.

The gin was a smash hit. We supplied it exclusively to Keystone (owner of The Rook) venues for 12 months while also selling an allocation direct to our growing database of thirsty gin fans. Critically, it demonstrated that Australia's on-premise had a serious local partner on its side—a gin-maker who did things that the big internationals simply couldn't do (or, perhaps just as relevantly, couldn't be bothered to do for a market as small as Australia). This sense of there being a new disruptive player on the scene became seriously real with our next Bartender Series release.

On 9 June 2015, Qantas announced that Rockpool Group, led by the brilliant Neil Perry, would be taking over leadership for food and drinks everywhere from its lounges to its in-flight service. We'd already started to build a relationship with Qantas, with our gins served in their first-class lounges, but this was an opportunity to take this modern Australian relationship to the next level. It took Stu exactly a day to see what that opportunity could be: a Bartender Series gin made with Neil's Rockpool Group mixologists and served exclusively in Qantas lounges and across the Rockpool Group venues. Cam and I agreed instantly, and Stu went to work connecting the dots to set up the opportunity.

It didn't take long. The Qantas beverage team and Rockpool's top bartenders, led by Beverage Manager Ryan Gavin, joined Stu and Cam for a day of distillation in mid-October. Cameron already had big ideas for the gin he wanted to make, inspired by Neil Perry's introduction of Chinese flavours into modern Australian cooking. Again, the sense of our in-built advantages as a local, craft-making–led gin producer becomes clear when you read the email Cam sent to the Qantas and Rockpool folks in advance of the session:

Just thought I'd send through a list of some of the botanicals I have sourced for Monday. We don't need to use them all, but I thought I'd send a list for everyone to get their head around:

- *Java long pepper*

- *cinnamon quills*

- *prickly ash (green Sichuan)*
- *red Sichuan*
- *honey suckle*
- *chrysanthemum*
- *Chinese red dates (grown in Mildura)*
- *grains of paradise*
- *oolong tea*
- *Pu'er tea*
- *black pepper*
- *macadamia nuts*
- *cubeb*
- *cardamom*
- *coriander seed*
- *lemon myrtle*
- *Tasmanian pepperberry*
- *Angelica root*
- *lavender*
- *green cardamom*
- *cassia*
- *things from the garden....rosemary, bay leaf, olive leaf, kaffir lime leaf, etc.*
- *juniper (of course!)*
- *apples and citrus (I have some grapefruit growing at home along with some great lemons).*

No wonder everyone wanted to make gin with us. Imagine being a bartender and receiving an email like that from a world-class distillery. This was dreamland stuff, and once again, the result was a cracking new gin.

We released Modern Australian Gin to the public in December 2015 in time to celebrate our second birthday as a brand. It was just two years since the launch of Four Pillars, and the release of Rare Dry Gin, and we were already announcing the fifth gin to join the family (and the second in our limited-edition Bartender Series).

With these first two Bartender Series partnerships we set the tone for a decade of collaborative gin-making. We partnered with people who knew drinks and had great flavour ideas, like Jimmy Irvine, the wildly talented bartender who got Stu to go foraging for seaweed with him. Together, we made a quirky little gin called Underground Sydney Gin, before later hiring him to become our first creative drinks director. But that's a whole other chapter.

We also partnered with people who ran brilliant hospitality businesses ranging from the beer- and music-inspired Sticky Carpet Gin we made to celebrate the reopening of the grand old Espy Hotel in Melbourne's St Kilda (scene of some of teenage Cameron's formative nights watching his brother play in a number of Melbourne's iconic bands) to the pair of Midday and Midnight Gins we made to celebrate the Merivale family's iconic venues in Sydney's drinks scene. We made small runs of gins to celebrate the reopening of Peter Gilmore's Quay (QQQQ Gin – a rare example of us breaking our three-word gin-name protocol) and the tenth birthday of Coda in Melbourne. And we partnered with modern Australian icons, such as the chocolate makers at Koko Black, the body scrub legends at Frank Body and (arguably, the most iconic of all) the skincare and storytelling geniuses at Go-To Skincare.

Each of these collaborations had multiple impacts throughout our business and our brand. Each new gin gave us a new story to tell, a new process to celebrate, a new drink to share. Plus, each new collaborator gave us access to a fresh audience and fanbase (and by choosing our partners carefully, we always found an audience that was glad to meet Four Pillars). Lastly, each partnership and launch was an excuse for a party, an experience, an activation, an event or a pop-up, like the Negroni store we launched in Flinders Lane, Melbourne, to celebrate Negroni Week at Garden State, or like the gin dinners we hosted across QT venues to celebrate the release of our collaborative Ordered Chaos Gin.

But, perhaps most influential of all was our decision to collaborate with other craft gin distillers around the world. On face value, we might have seen these other craft gin-makers as competitors, but it was pretty obvious to us that we all had a common enemy (big, global gin brands and their corporate owners) and we all had lots in common (a desire to craft delicious gins that were unique to our places in the world), so why not trade ideas and create something special together? Plus, Cam fancied the idea of being able to write off a trip to Europe as a tax-deductible work expense, so our Distiller Series was born.

First up was the Santamania distillery in Madrid, where Cam combined our signature Australian botanicals with their passion for more savoury notes to make Cousin Vera's Gin (they also had a CARL still, called Vera, and she was so similar to Wilma that we reckoned they must be cousins). From Spain, we moved to Sweden where Jon Hilgren's Hernö distillery was making (we thought) the best gin in the northern hemisphere. The result was Dry Island Gin, with the blue-and-yellow label earning it the nickname 'the Ikea gin' from many of our customers. From there we went to Japan and made Changing Seasons Gin with Alex Davies, the master distiller at The Kyoto Distillery. It was Alex who introduced Cameron to the power and flavour of yuzu (an East Asian citrus), leading first to a Rare Dry Gin variation using fresh Victorian yuzu and then later to our sensational Fresh Yuzu Gin, now part of the Four Pillars permanent range.

We released Changing Seasons Gin just as the first Australian Covid lockdowns were taking hold. And the ongoing challenges of Covid meant that our next Distiller Series collaboration (with Stranger & Sons of Goa in India) had to be conducted entirely over Zoom. The result of all the trading of botanical ideas over the interwebs and through the postal system was Spice Trade Gin. And then, with travel privileges returned, we finally made it over to visit Tom Warner at Warner's Gin in sunny Northamptonshire, where we agreed to trade some of our iconic Shiraz fruit in return for some of his signature rhubarb. The result (our most recent Distiller Series) was Green Apple & Rhubarb Gin, where we added fresh apples, a distillery-made apple juice and a distillery-made apple cider to create a gin that was like an apple crumble in a glass.

Looking back at all the awards we have won over the past five years, I believe that, while our bartender and brand collaborations drove huge growth for our brand in Australia, it's been these collaborations with other craft distillers and gin-makers that has helped cement Four Pillars' reputation as, arguably, the most influential craft gin producer in the world right now.

But, before we could get to that, we needed to turn all this collaboration and innovation into a business model for growth. We needed what I call a theory of brand success.

DRINKS BREAK NO.3:
The Negroni

The Negroni really is the ultimate story in a glass. Legend has it that, in 1919, Count Camillo Negroni walked into Caffe Casoni, a Florence bar, after a particularly bad day. His usual drink was an Americano (the cocktail, not the coffee), which in turn was a riff on the now-forgotten classic, the Milano-Torino (the drink, not the bike race).

The Count ordered his usual Americano, but asked them to leave out the soda water (which would only water his drink down) and instead strengthen it with a shot of gin. This became his new regular order, and soon other people were walking into the bar and saying, 'I'll have a Negroni too'. The legend of the Negroni was born, the ultimate equal parts, perfectly balanced, bittersweet and boozy cocktail.

I first came across the Negroni, alongside other classic cocktails like the Blood and Sand, at the iconic bar Milk and Honey in London in the early 2000s (see page 16 for more on that). Rebecca had a much more sophisticated palate than me, so she was the one ordering all the bittersweet grown-up drinks. What I didn't realise was that I was witnessing the beginnings of a revival in classic early twentieth-century cocktails that would directly influence the craft gin boom that was to follow.

No.1: Negroni (and Contessa)

30 ml Four Pillars Gin
30 ml Campari
30 ml sweet vermouth
Orange
Ice

The Negroni is not only (arguably) the greatest cocktail of all time, but also the easiest to make. I prefer it café style, meaning the drink is served simply in a low tumbler or rocks glass over ice with a slice of orange. The drink itself is equal parts gin, Campari and sweet vermouth. Start by pouring 30 ml, 30 ml, 30 ml or batch up a whole bottle to keep in the fridge.

Vermouth with a twist

I love this drink both with our classic Rare Dry Gin and our dedicated Spiced Negroni Gin. Experiment with different sweet vermouths: some are more herbaceous and complex than others. My preferences are Cocchi or Antica Formula. You can also experiment with other bitter alternatives to Campari. Using Aperol instead of Campari gives you a softer, less bitter drink known as a Contessa. Go further and use Lillet Blanc and Suze from France and you've got yourself a white Negroni.

No.2: Milano-Torino (and Americano)

45 ml Campari
45 ml sweet red vermouth
Soda water
Ice

As I touched on in the story behind the drink, the Negroni had some illustrious precursors. First came the Milano-Torino, an equal parts Italian café concoction of Campari (from Milano) and sweet vermouth (from Torino). It drinks like a lighter, less boozy Negroni. American visitors to Italy often found their Milano-Torino too strong (or perhaps they were just suffering from the summer heat). Either way they would ask for it to be lengthened with some soda water. As happened with espresso coffee lengthened with the addition of hot water, Italians called both drinks an Americano.

Make your Milano-Torino with equal parts Campari and sweet red vermouth (45 ml of each would be ideal) in a short glass with lots of ice. Or top up 30 ml of each with soda water in a tall glass with ice to make it a lower alcohol and highly refreshing Americano.

So I cheated...

Neither of these drinks are technically gin drinks, but they're perfect aperitifs for the Negroni lover looking to start a summer's evening with something lower in alcohol.

No.3: Bijou

40 ml gin
40 ml sweet vermouth
20 ml Chartreuse
Orange bitters (optional)
Maraschino cherry
Ice

The world of equal parts cocktails is a deliciously simple one to explore. A favourite of mine is the Bijou, which swaps out the Campari in a Negroni and replaces it with green Chartreuse. I tend to vary the classic equal-thirds ratios and instead use 40 ml gin, 40 ml sweet vermouth and just 20 ml Chartreuse.

A Bijou is best served 'up', meaning in a cocktail or Nick and Nora (stem) glass with no ice. Stir the gin, sweet vermouth and green Chartreuse over ice until nice and cold (feel free to add a couple of dashes of orange bitters). Strain into a cocktail glass and garnish with a twist and or maraschino cherry.

Watch out as this drink can be both very sweet and very boozy. Also try a version where you swap the Chartreuse for Grand Marnier. Have fun experimenting!

No.4: Jasmine (and Bloody Jasmine)

20 ml Bloody Shiraz Gin
20 ml Campari
20 ml dry curacao (or any other orange liqueur, such as Cointreau)
20 ml fresh lemon juice
Orange bitters
Lemon peel
Ice

Another bittersweet classic, this one works equally well with Rare Dry Gin or Bloody Shiraz Gin (making it a Bloody Jasmine). Our perfect recipe for a Bloody Jasmine is Bloody Shiraz Gin, Campari, dry curacao (or any other orange liqueur, such as Cointreau), fresh lemon juice and a dash of orange bitters. Stir down over ice, strain into a cocktail glass and garnish with a twist or disc of lemon peel.

Always a classic

The Jasmine is considered a modern classic (invented in California in the 1990s), but for me, it fits perfectly into the lineage of simple, balanced, Campari-powered, bittersweet cocktails that date back to the Negroni.

FOURTEEN

A gin-fuelled content rocket

By being clear that our total focus should be on the craft of making better and different gin (or, more accurately, gins), we had defined both an aesthetic and a tone of voice for the brand (in everything from the custom-made bottle to our labels).

And then, in thinking about how we could grow the Four Pillars business, our maker instincts had led us to collaborate with like-minded partners, further stimulating our creativity and giving rise to yet more gins (and yet more Made From Gin products, like the incredible Gin Pigs). We had developed an approach to crafting our storytelling and we had more than enough craft-led stories to tell. The fundamentals of our business system were in place. Now we needed to build the brand/bias system to help grow that business. And it was going to be a brand system built on craft intimacy.

The way I see it, every business operates within the context of a system, and every business is itself a system. There are things it does within that system to drive sales and make money, and things it does to make friends and build loyalty and brand. Sometimes those are the same things, and sometimes it's a balancing act between competing priorities.

Within that system, every business manages tensions and faces choices. As I sit here typing today in 2024, we're sold in pretty much every good retail store, bar and restaurant in Australia. We're available in about 30 markets overseas and are one of the most successful craft gin brands in the world when it comes to airport and cruise ship duty-free. We also have a magnificent home that welcomes around 200 000 visitors every year, plus a beautiful drinks-led brand experience in Sydney. And we have around 150 staff working across our business. Our intimacy-led model that values smallness has actually scaled into a business that sells as much gin as Hendrick's in Australia (remember Hendrick's had around 60 per cent of the super-premium gin market in Australia when we first began).

How did this happen? How did all these pieces of the system we built fit together? What drove what? How did success (and growth) in one area contribute to success in another? Which parts of the system were the ends (the real point of the whole thing) and which were the means (the enablers that allowed us to grow the kind of business we wanted to grow)? And what did this system demand of us in terms of creativity, design, storytelling, experiences, culture, leadership, values and so on?

Understanding how a system like this works and grows can be captured in what I call a theory of brand success. To make the most of the potential of any business, we need to develop a working model that can help anchor our thinking—a theory we can believe in. Here's what we quickly figured out for Four Pillars in our first couple of years.

- As a business, we wanted to be famous for our making—both for the gins we made and for the craft, passion and attention to detail that went into exploring gin and all its flavour possibilities. To achieve that goal, we needed to be good at telling those stories and that meant being journalists and curators of our own business stories, capturing and telling those stories in real time. We needed to have strong writing and storytelling capabilities in house.

- Bringing our making and craft to life would require more than words, so we over-invested in photography, bringing in great photographers as often as we could afford to do so and buying a decent camera to capture content at the Distillery ourselves.

- As we made more gins, we needed to be able to bring their different personalities, flavour profiles and drinks possibilities to life, so we developed an approach to what we called 'lifestyle' photography that was more editorial than advertising. In other words, we created content as though our bottles and drinks were being shot for a beautiful fashion magazine cover and not for an advertisement. This was hardly an original thought —luxury fashion brands have been creating content like this for years—but in the world of spirits, it felt fresh and exciting. Quickly, the quality, colour, creativity and appeal of our content became a signature for Four Pillars and a clue to the quality, flavour, creativity and deliciousness of our gins and the drinks you could make with them.

- The rhythm of our communications was dictated by the rhythm of our gin-making. For example, in April/May we'd be talking about the latest Yarra Valley Shiraz vintage. In June we'd be talking about the Bloody Shiraz Gin we'd just released. Over the winter months we'd be talking about Negronis and getting ready to celebrate Negroni Week. In November we'd retell the story of Australian Christmas Gin and announce that year's label artist. Then in December we'd be getting ready for a summer of celebrating our signature Rare Dry Gin and its perfect serve in a G&T with orange. In February we'd typically have a limited collab release to celebrate. And all this, along with a bunch of smaller releases, events, partnerships and happenings, would mean that we always had something new to talk about and (critically) something new to sell to our growing database of gin lovers. Our brand was growing, supporting the growth of our brand in the trade through marketing investments that were mostly also giving us a return on the bottom line. Win-win!

The system sounds simple enough, but it was hugely complex and time consuming. Most gin brands had one or two products in their range. Here we were launching four or five different products every year. And each one needed stunning packaging, a gin story, a making and botanical backstory, a range of signature drinks, a beautiful content shoot, a detailed and beautifully crafted web page, a range of collateral (media material), a PR blitz and a launch event.

At first, all of this was coordinated and driven by Rebecca, but over time we began to grow our in-house team, bringing in roles around social media, events, design and content creation that, typically, would have sat with third-party agencies. We believed that our creativity, our speed and our ability to own and drive the brand in-house was a competitive advantage and an extension of our maker DNA. No one, we reasoned, would ever understand Four Pillars like Four Pillars people, so while our growth increasingly required us to bring in specialist partners in certain areas (most notably Liquid Ideas for PR and Weave for high-end creative design and content creation), we never relinquished ultimate creative control of our brand to an agency.

Not only did we resist the temptation to hand the keys to our brand to an agency, but we were scrupulous at making sure it always felt like the makers were in charge (which was an easy job as they were!). That meant never allowing our customers to detect the hand of the marketing team at work with clever copy, opportunistic promotions or bullshit claims. Instead, we made sure that everything felt like a curated and polished version of the truth of what was happening in Healesville.

A great example of this was our social media community management. We prided ourselves on replying to every single comment, post, review or complaint across any social media channel. And for years, that was done mostly from Sydney by either me, Rebecca or Ebony (our first hire in the marketing space). Even though we were often replying from an office or kitchen table in Sydney, we always replied as though we were sitting in the Distillery next to Cam and Wilma. And years later, as we were able to scale our social and customer service teams, we remained committed to that geographic intimacy between our production teams and our social and customer teams. The result is that when you're talking to Four Pillars you are really talking to Four Pillars, not to an outsourced or dislocated marketing, customer service or social media team. Intimacy means intimacy!

Looking at our growing commitment to sustainability in recent years, this model has once again come to the fore. The more we have done to eliminate water, energy and packaging waste from our business, the more stories we've had to tell. And that storytelling has helped drive new levels of engagement and brand loyalty among our customers (because our deliciously better gins are now better for the planet too), meaning that our sustainability efforts are benefiting our bottom line as well as our local environment. Once again, that's the kind of win-win that we've built our brand around.

Our first events followed this same pattern. Cameron would make space in his small gin cage to host some gin fans in Warrandyte, while Rebecca and I made friends with the team at Workshop, a cool hipster space in Sydney, and arranged to start running gin workshops there (hosted by Stu). These events, alongside the more and more frequent events we were co-hosting with bars and partners in the trade, all gave us even more fuel for our storytelling. They allowed us to teach people how to enjoy Four Pillars while also showcasing what was becoming a key part of our brand: that we took our gin seriously, but not ourselves, and that we were committed to making great gin while also having a great deal of fun.

The more we grew, the more we tried to bring this energy to both sides of our growth, with Rebecca and I championing the direct engagement of our end consumers, and Stu and his key lieutenant Jen Bailey (who now runs the Four Pillars business in the USA) driving our engagement of the drinks trade alongside our distribution partners at Vanguard. Our objectives were the same: value individual experiences and relationships, create bias and loyalty towards our business and our gins, share our gin craft proudly but with humility, partner constantly (knowing our job was to bring the gin and the drinks to other people's parties), create stories for us to tell in our own social channels and inspire others to tell stories about us.

But, while this system and this theory worked well, it was clear that it would need one more piece to achieve real lift-off. Our business and our brand would need a permanent home.

USEFUL BIT #10:
THEORY OF BRAND SUCCESS

Okay, so this is where I need to double-down on an early caveat—everything in this Useful Bit is wrong. Every single word. For three reasons.

First, because I don't know your business, so I can only talk in general terms about brand success. It's up to you to figure out what is relevant and useful.

Second, because so many other elements matter that I won't have space to touch on here, such as nailing your product and packaging, your distribution and route to market, your approach to sales and service.

Third, because I have no data beyond my own experiences, and I am heavily biased. While this Useful Bit is about helping you come up with your own theory of brand growth, I will inevitably nudge you towards thinking my way. And that may not be the right way for you.

So, with all that said, let's try to identity and isolate the role you need your brand, creativity and marketing to play in helping you achieve your goals. In other words:

Why do you need to focus on your brand?

To work through this, we're going to set up two ideas: first, how brands help businesses; second, what builds brands.

The role of your brand in building your business

Back in Useful Bit #6, we went deep and looked at the role of feelings and emotions, and now it's time to take a zoomed-out view of the brand. My view (and, remember, this is just my view) is that we live in a world of abundance, so we don't

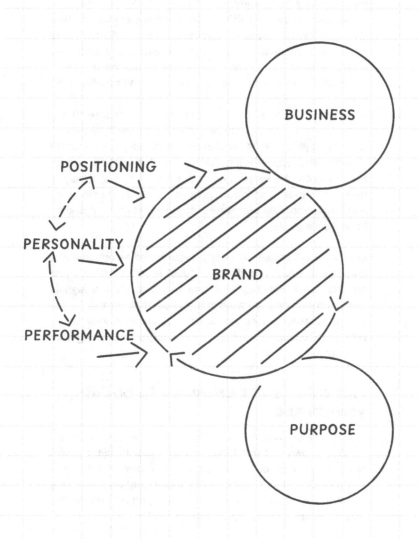

need *another* anything. But we can always benefit from a *better* something.

The first, and most powerful way to build a strong brand (remembering that 'brand' is simply a word for positive bias) is to make a powerfully differentiated and better product. But, that alone is not enough. History is littered with examples of 'better' products losing out to inferior alternatives, sometimes, of course, due to challenges around pricing or distribution, but other times simply due to brand preference.

My view of the role of a brand is simply to ensure that a business, product or service gets the credit it deserves. Seen through this lens, marketing, advertising, PR, political strategy and speechwriting (all areas I've worked in over the years) can be seen as noble pursuits, seeking simply to make sure that good ideas, politics, products, businesses and even people get discovered, appreciated and the chance to be successful.

In short, don't think of working on your brand as optional (it's not) or only necessary if your product is inferior (that's just not the case). Ensuring that your brand sends the signals you need to send, conveys the values that drive you and your business, and connects emotionally with your target customer/consumer/user are critical parts of building your core business.

The role of experiences in building your brand

Consider your own brand preferences. They could be for things you own and use frequently (like your favourite brand of running shoes) or things you aspire to own one day (like a luxury sports car). Where did those preferences come from? How did they form? Have they changed over time? How powerfully do you hold those preferences?

Then consider specialist categories like baby strollers, a category full of brands you've never heard of until you're expecting a baby. Then, suddenly, your social feed is full of them. Or, if you start up a business and have to decide whether to run the business on Google's workplace ecosystem or Microsoft 365, whether to host your website on Microsoft's Azure Cloud or AWS, whether to build your new store on Shopify or Big Commerce. Again, think about how you went about gathering information and learning about categories and brands that were previously not on your radar. Reflecting on how we ourselves form our preferences is a useful reminder of what can move the needle for our own businesses.

Or consider your weekly trip to the supermarket (if you still do the shopping old-school, bricks-and-mortar style): which brands do you choose? In which instances do you choose the product on special and in which categories is there a brand that you purchase consistently with absolute loyalty and minimal price sensitivity?

I believe that when we're talking about brands and loyalty, we're really just talking about biases and behaviours. We're talking about both attitudes (stated preferences) and behaviours (actual purchases). We're talking about the stories people tell themselves, often based on very limited knowledge about the product or category in question. We're talking about decisions that are irrational, but heavily rationalised. Where do these preferences, these biases, these instinctive responses come from?

Are these choices shaped by the stories these brands tell about themselves? In part, of course, which is why Useful Bit #9 focused on getting your story right. Are they shaped by how these brands look and feel? Absolutely, which is why Useful Bit #6 focused on helping you define how you want your business to feel. But there's also something bigger going on here.

The most important stories are the ones your customers tell themselves and the stories they are told by other people they trust (friends, colleagues, influencers and experts). To put it in marketing terms, it's the media we earn that really matters, not the media we pay for. And the media we earn is driven primarily by the things we do and the experiences we create.

The final part of our brand playbook needs to be a focus on the experiences we create for the people who matter most to us.

Putting it all together in a theory of brand success

Too many businesses focus on targeting everyone. But by targeting everyone, you're really targeting no one. How could you focus your efforts to have the maximum impact on the most engaged customers, the customers who can go on to become the greatest influencers and advocates for your business?

Many brands focus on talking to new customers. But the best chance you have to really engage customers is by targeting the ones you already have. How could you focus your efforts on delighting the customers you already have, building a narrow but deep well of customer loyalty that you can then expand over time? Almost as importantly, how could you focus all your new customer acquisition efforts on one narrow, highly targeted group (they might be unified by where they live or a passion they share). This laser focus on the quality (not quantity) of your customer engagement can help you build intensity, loyalty and advocacy into your brand.

Only you know how large your customer base needs to get and how quickly for your business to be viable. All I can offer you is a perspective on valuing intimacy more, valuing depth of engagement more, believing in the power of loyalty and advocacy more, and in trusting that mattering a lot to a few people is more important in the long term than being vaguely known by many.

Your theory of brand success is about creating a clear picture of the touchpoints of maximum impact for your business and your brand. What things can you commit to that can drive sales, engagement and brand loyalty and stimulate advocacy and growth?

Thinking in this way may help you focus on customer service and brand experience more, and on new customer acquisition, paid advertising and performance advertising less. But, remember, this is your brand and your success we're talking about. So, ultimately, finding the right balancing act is up to you. The key, once you have a theory, is to commit to it. Not every impact will be instantly measurable (the cult of short-term measurement is real and dangerous), but you'll be able to get a read pretty fast on whether the theory is working or not.

FIFTEEN

Home is where the gin is

Today there's a lot of debate (far too much debate) about the value of brands, about the difference between brand marketing and performance or growth marketing. If you're starting or growing a business, I have no doubt that you have multiple, conflicting voices in your ear telling you you're either investing too little or too much in this nebulous, intangible thing called your brand. But, as my old mentor Tara Back would always say, here's the thing...

The whole point of focusing on your brand is to be better. Better in your product, your service and the value you create for your customers. Better in your experiences, your imagery and your aesthetics. Better in your storytelling and the emotions you inspire in others. Better in ways that do the marketing for you. Better in ways that inspire others to share your story.

Within six months of launching Four Pillars it was obvious that, thanks to Cam and Stu and no thanks to me, we were making better gin (better, frankly, by every measure... from the quality and purity of the spirit to the approachability, appeal, aromatics and flavour of the gin).

Now making 'better' gin might not have been a huge problem that needed to be solved in the grand scheme of things (and, prior to 2013, few people knew they were missing a great citrus-forward, modern Australian gin from their lives), but nonetheless we had reached base camp—we had product advantage that we could now build a business around.

It was this core product advantage that made our intimacy-led approach to marketing and storytelling so powerful, but where it really came to life was when we opened our doors to the public and let people come and meet us, taste our gins and meet Wilma. We did it for the first time on World Gin Day 2014 and again on World Gin Day in 2015.

Looking back now it's remarkable to me that there was never any question among us three founders (or us six founders, really, as all six of us had our houses on the line for this one) that we should buy and develop a home for Four Pillars. One of our big questions was: why build a home so soon in the life of our little business? Once again, we were building our brand's future before we had got close to realising the potential of the present.

We'd made an offer on a home for Four Pillars, purchasing an old timber yard at 2A Lilydale Road in Healesville. While Rebecca and Sally had been lending their professional expertise and experience to Four Pillars for some time, now it was Leah Mackenzie's time to shine. Once again, we had won the lottery when it came to our founder group because we were about to build our brand home, and our distiller's wife was a brilliantly talented and highly pragmatic building project manager with a huge passion for architecture and design. Now, if we could just figure out how to pay for it, our brand was going to get its first proper home.

Had we followed the lessons of gin brands all over the world, we would have pressed on with making our gin in Rob's shed (or perhaps we wouldn't have bothered with the hassle of distilling at all and would have found someone to make gin for us). In that alternate universe, we would have focused all our efforts and all our available dollars on marketing, distribution and sales—perhaps we might even have grown faster for a bit. But, eventually, the world would have caught up with us because, beneath it all would have been a lack of substance. We would have been a gin brand, not the layered, committed gin-making business we are.

In this alternate reality, our ability to be defined by making, experimenting and innovating would have been severely limited. Likewise, our ability to place intimacy and experiences at the heart of our brand would have disappeared, and with it all our collaborative efforts with bartenders, distillers and brands. In short, the decision to create a home for Four Pillars was obviously right to us as we looked forward from those early start-up days, and it's equally obvious and right looking back a decade later. It's a rare example where foresight and hindsight were both 20:20. And it came from a willingness (once again) to reject the established playbook for spirits. Instead, we took our cues from brands we admired in other industries.

There are inherent risks as a start-up business in looking to replicate the playbooks and successes of big, iconic brands and success stories. But there's also huge value in being able to anchor the logic of your own playbook (your theory of brand success) to lessons and examples from others who are further down the path. The key is to both learn the right lessons and to figure out which of those lessons could be most valuable to you. For me, as I developed the strategies and ideas for how Four Pillars would grow, two brands jumped out again and again: Aesop and Apple.

While operating in very different categories, this Melbourne-founded skincare maker and the Californian computing powerhouse have something critical in common. They both value design, aesthetics, tactility and materials enormously, and use that commitment to send signals to design-loving people that their products are worth more. Neither discount their products much (if ever) and both (here comes the relevant lesson) have anchored their brand storytelling in their own physical homes.

The first Apple store opened in 2001 just outside of Washington D.C. The first Aesop store opened only three years later in the Melbourne suburb of St Kilda. In both cases, the stores opened before the rise of social media, so we hadn't yet seen the full amplifying effects of social media and smartphones on physical experiences. And, yet, here were two brands, one already a global computing brand but getting ready to disrupt the phone category, the other a start-up skincare brand that had emerged from a hair salon, both of whom were hitching their future growth to the power of bricks-and-mortar experiences.

Aesop and Apple did this at a time when the accepted wisdom was that you purchased your luxury skincare products from counters in department stores, and you purchased your mobile phones from the phone companies. In building their own stores, they were disrupting the retail models of their categories and selling direct to their consumers. Plus, they were diverting what could have been sizable marketing budgets into the costs of fitting out and staffing physical stores. Why? What did they see that the rest of their competitors didn't? Doubtless the real answer to this question is complex and multifaceted, but I want to focus on two key elements: signalling and service.

We had already reflected on the importance of signalling for our gin business when developing the primary design elements of our Rare Dry Gin bottle and label. We were determined to take every opportunity to convey the right visual cues (quality, flavour and timeless craft delivered with modern Australian personality) through all the existing touchpoints available to us. What both Apple and Aesop grasped was the need to not just take advantage of existing touchpoints (think about the perfectly crafted design and copy on every piece of Aesop packaging or the pleasure of unboxing an Apple product), but to invent new touchpoints that could themselves become powerful signals of their values.

Apple stores have always been beacons of calm, considered design in a noisy world. One of the things I look for in every multi-level Apple store is the staircase. Perhaps best exemplified by the extraordinary staircase beneath an iconic glass cube that takes you to the subterranean Fifth Avenue store in New York City, Apple uses its care and attention to detail around its stores (and its staircases) to send the signal that Apple comes from a place that values design, engineering and attention to detail. As you stand there considering whether the iPhone, iPad or MacBook in front of you is really worth the premium over the Android/Windows alternatives, there's Apple's design language sending you the clear signal that this stuff is designed and made better. Plus (and here's the real kicker), choosing an Apple product will also go on to say something about you, your choices and your values.

In other words, by creating stores that send a powerful signal, Apple has built a brand and product family that, in turn, help their customers send a powerful signal about themselves. Apple has helped build being an Apple user into a form of identity, and weaving your business and your product into someone's identity is the ultimate form of bias and loyalty.

Aesop stores are much the same. Although far smaller than Apple stores, they receive just as much design attention. Always in the right neighbourhoods, every store is a unique interior architecture response to the environment and culture that surrounds it. And inside, branding is kept to a minimum, with the heavy lifting done by the beautiful, repeating display of product. In Aesop's case, its stores communicate its values around quiet luxury, product excellence, thoughtful design and a more aesthetically pleasing world. Its stores embody the aesthetic values of the kinds of people it seeks to attract, leveraging every sensory element, with products smelling as beautiful as they look and, typically, an artistic window display (a winning strategy for luxury brands since Leïla Menchari was turning the Hermès windows on rue du Faubourg Saint-Honoré in Paris into must-see attractions).

Which brings us to service and Aesop's focus on sinks and scents. Every Aesop store is different, but every store has one thing in common: a working sink. The sink says this is a place where product and product trial is everything. This is a place to experience our products, and our staff are skin experts and consultants. Our products are better, and we simply want you to discover which ones are right for you. This approach translated over to the fragrance space when Aesop, finally, after years of product development, moved into this hugely challenging space dominated by the big luxury houses. Purchase something from Aesop today and your products will be placed in a beautiful cloth bag that is then sprayed with one of their fragrances before the staff members walks around to your side of the counter and hands it to you. This act of graceful service helps you forget about how much you just paid and means that the fragrance of Aesop lingers with you and your purchase for days to come.

Apple's use of their stores to offer Genius Bar services and product seminars while displaying their products exactly as they wish is a very different model to Aesop's. But the logic is the same: they simply could not send the signals they send or offer the service they do without anchoring their brands in their own bricks-and-mortar homes.

In thinking about the importance of their homes, both as a physical signal of their brand values and their brand experiences and as a springboard for their approach to service and customer experiences,

Apple and Aesop were acting as what I think of as *experience brands*. Businesses where experiences are not just used to tell a story, they are used to inspire others to tell the story for you. Someone smarter and more original than me once described this as the difference between storytelling and storydoing (refer back to page 78 for more on this). Apple and Aesop both 'do' the story they want others to 'tell' about them. Why should gin (or any category for that matter) be any different? Why wouldn't we focus on being and doing our story, and inspiring others (our customers and end users) to tell and share our story for us?

There's no place like home, our gin home.

Once we had secured our home, Leah started to think about the development, engaging a great local builder and finding some affordable architectural design support (we didn't have the budget to go all out with an architect so Leah had to bring a lot of the expertise herself...luckily, she was brilliant at it). Meanwhile, I got to work on a vision for what our home would need to be. Here's some of what we said in our brief:

Our four experience pillars

- The craft of distilling (distillery operation)
- The craft of cocktail making (tastings and masterclasses)
- Drink better, not more (retail)
- Modern Australian brand (hospitality and community)

Our target audiences

We need a space that welcomes and engages (in no particular order):

- Retail/bar buyers and owners
- Cocktail/industry influencers and tastemakers
- Retail/bar staff
- Passionate/loyal enthusiast customers
- Distilling geeks
- Visiting Yarra Valley food and wine tourists (local)

- Visiting Yarra Valley food and wine tourists (from overseas)
- Proud local neighbours and their friends/families.

Our brand design

Four Pillars makes a premium product, but with a deep commitment to craft. Our desire from the beginning has been to create a modern classic brand, proudly established in 2013, but timeless in its aesthetic. Our ambition has also been to create a modern Australian brand that represents the diversity and dynamism and confidence of modern Australia.

We are a brand that has its home in wine country, but is close to Melbourne, and our DNA is both rural and urban. Our aesthetic is full of these tensions: modern and classic; polished and craft; premium and functional. We also have a particular passion for rich photography—imagery that celebrates the two crafts we are built around: distilling and cocktail making.

Looking back, it's remarkable how much of that brief remains true and is exactly what we were trying to deliver (and grow) when we were developing the neighbouring site on Lilydale Road in 2021. Once again, we saw the enormous benefits of being aligned, both on the strategy for our business as well as on the nuances of how we wanted our brand to show up in the world.

We opened the doors to Four Pillars Distillery in Healesville in late 2015. A soft opening to locals was followed by a grand opening party over the Melbourne Cup long weekend. This would become our official Australian Christmas Gin launch weekend in the future (like World Gin Day, another day that will forever be marked in the Four Pillars family calendar).

Anson Smart had once again dropped everything to join Rebecca down in Healesville and take sensational photos of the whole place. Sally and the Liquid Ideas team were drumming up a stack of great media coverage. And Scotty Gauld and the launch team were ready with open gin bottles and open arms. Many of them are still with us today, including big Elton our tasting bench legend. Elton, like Scotty and Michelle (our first-ever employee, who started part-time doing the books for Cam to keep him out of jail, and who now runs the whole Healesville show), now has a still named after his mum.

The coverage said exactly what we hoped ...

It's the embodiment of Healesville's modern-era transformation: what was a scrappy timber merchant is now a bespoke gin distillery.
Good Food (SMH and Age), 12 October 2015

It's literally a Willy Wonka factory for gin-loving adults.
Concrete Playground, 23 October 2015

Scott and team had done an amazing job of getting the place ready for the grand opening weekend and the place was buzzing. From day one, the team were a well-grooved, gin-slinging hospitality machine. We were up and running. At first, we decided to only open our doors from Thursdays to Mondays, but very quickly it became clear we had seven days a week of traffic and custom on our hands.

We kept the food offering simple (bringing in guest food trucks for the weekend); focused the drinks on gin; gave the best tasting experiences we could think of; offered our gins in G&Ts, cocktails and (critically) mini G&T paddles; put together a simple retail offering; and hosted as many masterclasses and immersive sessions as we could. Of all the things that defined what we created at the Distillery and the impact it had on our business, four really stand out.

1. Built-in brilliance

People are everything in business, especially when you're small and growing fast. We were lucky to have so many great people not just in our team, but in our three founding couples. Leah took total ownership not just of the project to transform the old shed into our home, but of the ongoing maintenance of every little detail from the floral and botanical displays that gave the space warmth and life to the growing gardens and foliage on the facade of the Distillery. Great people who bring both expertise and ownership to their work are an irreplaceable asset and in this case we had one of the best of them in Leah.

Two other points are worth making. First that, yes, bringing ownership to your work is easier when the person in question is literally a co-owner of the business. But it's also about autonomy, purpose, support and joy. I'd like to think that, for the most part, we gave Leah the balance of support and autonomy to get on with doing what she could do (and none of the three co-founders could do). And, I'd also like to think that we'd built a brand that was both greatly invested in its purpose and also great fun. And that made going above and beyond (as we all did over that first decade) that bit more motivating and joyful.

The second point is that it can be easy to discount the power of the skills you've got because they are, literally in this case, in the family. There's sometimes a need to bring in outside expertise (at great expense) to supplement the knowledge and skills you have in house. In my view, we could have searched far and wide and never found two people as capable and perfectly suited to Four Pillars and our needs in those early days than Leah and Rebecca (Sally's credentials as our PR partner were never in question). So, while it's true that Rebecca had never worked in consumer marketing (let alone run all the marketing for a spirits brand) and Leah had never led a distillery development project, it's also true that they were without question the best people for the jobs.

2. People, culture and hospitality

If it's true that people are everything in general, it's doubly true when it comes to running a hospitality business. Hospitality, along with relationships, is one of Stu's great obsessions. For him it comes down to warmth, empathy, awareness, knowledge and generosity. I paraphrase because he could talk about the Stuart Gregor view on hospitality for literally days (inhospitable bartenders and arrogant sommeliers are high on his notorious 'hate list'). Meanwhile, down in Healesville, we were brilliantly served by Cam's ability to build a team that felt like a family, and his old mate Scott Gauld's ability to choreograph that family to deliver an exceptional and professional hospitality operation. Within a very short space of time, Four Pillars Distillery was known by visitors as the friendliest place with the best service in the Valley, and by hospo staff as the best place to work in the Valley.

3. Paddles and booklets

It seems like a small thing, but getting our drinks service right was a key part of shaping the brand experience at the Distillery. For one, we needed to have the confidence to only serve gin drinks and not a range of spirits. What if someone wanted a vodka and soda or a single malt whisky? The short answer was, they could try something similar with one of our gins, or they could go elsewhere (and we'd cheerfully recommend places to go). Likewise, we needed the confidence to charge for tastings when almost every winery in the area gave them away for free. Our logic was that people would value something more if they paid for it. Plus, by charging for tastings, we could afford to properly staff them and encourage our tastings stars like Elton to take much longer over them. Plus, we gave people the chance to redeem the cost of the tasting against the purchase of a bottle of gin, incentivising people to choose their favourite.

That sense of choosing which gin you liked most was at the heart of the most simple but critical experience innovation Scott and Cam introduced: the G&T tasting paddle. Three 15 ml pours of three gins, all served neat with our recommended garnish, with a small ice bucket and a bottle of Fever-Tree tonic on the side. This way people could curate their own mini tasting while enjoying the equivalent of one regular G&T. The impact was bigger than we imagined for three reasons.

First was the sense of theatre. Seeing paddles being delivered to a table made other tables immediately order the same. There's a contagious quality to anything delivered with theatre in a hospitality environment. Second was catering to drivers. The Yarra Valley remains hard to access from Melbourne without someone driving, so we have to responsibly cater to large numbers of drivers every week. By giving people the chance to enjoy a single drink responsibly while still having an experience with a range of gins, we'd solved a problem and created value for them.

Third was celebrating the diversity of gins we made with everyone who visited. By encouraging people to try three of our gins, each in a G&T, we trebled the chance of them falling in love with one of them and buying a bottle to take home. Converting visitation to bottle sales was a critical part of making money and turning a one-off experience into loyalty and repeat purchase.

This was also the logic behind the huge investment we would make in those early days in beautifully crafted Four Drinks brochures (four perfect serves for each gin) and cocktail books covering our whole family of gins and drinks styles (we ended up publishing a series of four of them, and to this day have people asking for copies). It was this investment in collateral that helped us turn the experience people were having in Healesville into an experience they could repeat at home. Without it, that one delicious Bloody Sour made for them by Scott's brilliant bar team might have turned into an unfinished bottle of Bloody Shiraz Gin at home that they didn't know what to do with.

4. Maker Sessions

Just as we trusted that great experiences in Healesville would turn into great drinks experiences at home that would go on to inspire people to purchase, serve, share and gift Four Pillars Gin more and more often, we also trusted in another critical driver of word of mouth: masterclasses.

Of all the various gin, cocktails and marmalade masterclasses we have run over the years, the one I am most proud of is the Maker Sessions. Moving into our own distillery home allowed us to both add a second production still (Jude) and also an experimental still (Eileen). Using Eileen, we hosted Maker Sessions once a month, where regular consumers could come and make a gin from scratch with Cameron, receiving a bottle of their creation a few weeks later. This wasn't a gin-blending class or some other half-cooked approach to bespoke gin-making, this was the real deal—loading Eileen with botanicals by hand and working with Cam on the recipe (usually using some new ingredient he was excited to trial that month).

For a business growing as fast as we were, tying up our master distiller once a month to take personal care of 12 consumers for a few hours might have seemed like overkill. But we took a different view. These were 12 people willing to pay for the chance to get hands-on and truly intimate with our craft, falling deeper in love with our brand. This kind of opportunity in our attention-deficit world was priceless and would drive a level of conviction, loyalty and exponential word of mouth that money simply could not buy.

With the Distillery flying over that first summer of 2015 and 2016, we started to face new problems of scale and growth. We had more opportunities coming our way than we knew what to do with (and we certainly didn't have the budgets or resources to say 'yes' to all of them). And we had a fast-growing team fielding a fast-growing range of enquiries about what was happening in Healesville. It became clear that we couldn't trade on the instincts of the three co-founders and our three spouses alone. We needed to formalise some of the principles behind the decisions we were making, and we needed to share that understanding of what was making Four Pillars tick with a fast-growing team.

SIXTEEN

Faith in the power of experiences (and word of mouth)

Istarted working professionally in 1997 in the UK. Terrestrial TV was still linear in format, and limited to five channels. Video shops were still in business, most people I knew didn't have a mobile phone, and I still bought a newspaper every day and collected magazines. With every passing decade of my working life, the media landscape has changed more than in the prior century. It's Moore's law of geometric progression in action, but here in the media landscape.

I was fortunate that my first professional communications role was in politics in the UK, where strict laws on political advertising meant that party conferences, speeches, press conferences and door-to-door campaigning were the bread and butter of political communications strategies. In other words, I learned my craft in a world that didn't rely on advertising, because it couldn't.

As I moved then into the brand space I became more and more convinced that, while storytelling and the curation of your story was a critical part of building a successful business (after all, if you don't take responsibility for your narrative, no one else will), the key was to then ensure that your story showed up in the experiences you created for the people who mattered to you. Because in a world of media clutter, constant noise, and shorter and shorter attention spans, it was experiences that would shape preferences and inspire purchase, loyalty and recommendation (the things that help brands grow).

The framework I developed to think about the kinds of experiences that move the needle on brand preference was based on the idea of *sandwiches* and *peacocks*. I unpack this in the next Useful Bit on page 174, but the short story is that it's about the twin ideas of convenience versus beauty, ease versus delight, being seamless versus standing out. Both matter, but in different amounts to different businesses (my beloved Apple and Aesop benchmarks are a case in point...both valuing aesthetics while both also focusing on delighting and helping their customers). And the key is to apply both to every touchpoint you control, every piece of what the marketing industry calls your 'owned' media.

Stu had developed a similar point of view about the media landscape. For him, it was all about the importance of the media you 'earn' (inspiring others to write about you) over the media you pay for. Stu also valued owned media (i.e. the things you own and control as a brand: from your home to your packaging to your digital presence) enormously too, but while I came at it from the point of view of the designed experience, he obsessed about it at a human level, ensuring that we always showed up with warmth, generosity, knowledge, charm and humility.

Between the two of us, we developed a very clear playbook for how we wanted Four Pillars to show up in the world, which I captured in the form of four clear principles for how we wanted people to feel every time they encountered our business in the world:

- We wanted people to feel we were the most *creative* brand in gin. That meant always exposing people to our passion for craft, making, innovating and experimenting that characterised our approach to making gin, making drinks and making creatively with partners in the world.

- We wanted people to feel we were the most *delicious* brand in gin. After all, creativity wasn't terribly important to people if it didn't translate into flavours they loved. Every touchpoint needed to communicate deliciousness and drinkability, showing that flavour (not just novelty for the sake of it) was always our top priority.

- We wanted people to feel we were the most *well-designed* brand in gin, not because we wanted them to think of us as aesthetic snobs or design wankers (although I may have been called both of those things a few times), but because a commitment to design would signal a wider commitment to attention to detail and to sweating the small stuff, caring about the stuff that goes unseen. Given that our gin-making happens out of sight of the majority of our drinks, this signal is critical to send.

- Lastly, we wanted people to feel we were the most *fun* brand in gin. This principle helped enshrine a key balancing act between my desire for the Four Pillars experience to always feel crafted, considered and high quality (i.e. worth paying more for) and Stu's fear that too much focus on everything being designed and considered could be a bit, well, boring and un-Australian. And as a modern Australian brand bringing flavour and disruption to the gin category, we could take the gin seriously, but we couldn't take ourselves seriously. After all, making and drinking gin is just about the most fun job in the world, so it should feel that way.

Perhaps more important than the principles were, once again, the people — both the kinds of people we hired and the way we trained them (warm, smart, energised people who we immersed in the world of gin and the world of Four Pillars) and the roles we prioritised (extra staff in the Distillery to offer hospitality and impromptu tastings table by table; full-time in-house people responding to every email, call, social media message and comment).

There is simply no way that a big corporate company or consultancy would have sanctioned our investment in people, but the reality is that it was the people and the experiences they delivered for our customers that made Four Pillars (the brand) what it was and what it remains today. If the gin was everything to us, then the craft-led brand experience we were wrapping around the gin was the extra layer of packaging that helped take our business to the next level.

USEFUL BIT #11:
BRAND EXPERIENCE PLAYBOOK

It should be clear at this stage in the book that I'm obsessed with experiences.

Which experiences will move the needle for your brand?

In answering this question and building out your brand experience playbook, we need to ask ourselves two more foundational sets of questions. The first will help you identify which experiences to focus on; the second will help you reflect on what a better experience might look like.

First, some questions about the touchpoints of maximum opportunity:

- Which touchpoints matter most to your customers? Are you at least meeting their expectations across all these interactions?

- Which points represent the best chance for you to differentiate your business from your competitors? Which give you the chance to stand out and be memorable?

- Which touchpoints make you money? How can you add a layer of brand experience excellence onto these transactions? How can you add value to your customer through experience, generosity or giving them something to talk about and share? This is critical, as brand-building that makes you money is the kind you can keep investing in.

- Which interactions have the greatest potential to win new customers and fans. Are you optimised to turn interactions into friendships there? What more or different could you do?

Second, we need to ask some more questions to help you focus on the types of experiences that will be most powerful across these touchpoints and interactions. But, first, we should talk a little about the thinking behind all this.

Reflect on your own experiences, brand preferences, sense of loyalty to certain businesses. There's something consistent about the experiences that change how we feel about a business, the experiences that keep us coming back again and again, the experiences that inspire us to recommend a business or a product to everyone we know. We remark about them to others because they are, quite literally, remarkable.

To simplify things, I've come to believe these experiences are remarkable in one of two ways. As I mentioned on page 172, I like to call them *sandwich* experiences and *peacock* experiences.

Sandwich convenience

Growing up as a teenager in the UK, I grew up in a world of white-bread sandwiches, usually filled with cheese, ham, egg or some kind of fish paste. The sandwich was rarely delightful, but always convenient. And convenience is what sandwich experience is all about.

When you're thinking about experiences with sandwich DNA, you're thinking about ease, speed, convenience, the removal of pain and friction for your customer, user or consumer. You're thinking about how you can be shockingly easier to use, remarkably easier to do business with and, conversely, how switching to an alternative would create far too much pain and friction to be worthwhile.

This is where the *shocking* point is key. Our loyalty and brand bias isn't moved by something that works a little better—it's when things are made transformatively easier and better. That's the power of sandwich thinking.

Peacock plumage

The peacock brings a very different perspective. I went to high school in Warwick, a beautiful town in the British Midlands and home to a stunning medieval castle with grounds full of

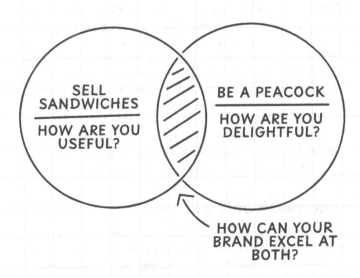

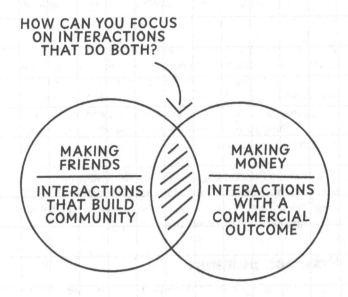

peacocks. On face value, the peacock's excessive plumage appears rather inconvenient and cumbersome, but it serves a hugely important biological purpose for the male peacock: it shows that it's so healthy and well-fed that it has been able to divert surplus energy into growing feathers.

A peacock's colourful feathers help it stand out and send a signal of biological advantage. Thinking like a peacock as a business asks you to stand out; to be colourful; to create desire and delight; to recognise that choosing you is not an entirely rational act; and to convey your values through design, aesthetics, experiences and behaviours. Thinking like a peacock gets you thinking about the signals you're sending about things people can't see (like your commitment to quality control) through the things people can see (your equivalent of plumage).

My colleagues at Four Pillars have heard me say this far too many times, but we live in a world dominated by sandwiches, where the likes of Amazon, Netflix and Uber have sought to bring shockingly frictionless ease to their categories. But within this sandwich-obsessed world, there's still room for peacocks to stand out, whether it's Aesop's commitment to beautifully designed stores and attention to detail or Liquid Death's renegade creativity showcasing its determination to disrupt the water category. Whether it's Gentle Monster's approach to its stores as art installations, placing creativity and aesthetics at the heart of its eyewear brand, or even the wildly creative, colourful window displays in every Hermès store around the world.

Where does your customer want you to serve up sandwiches? Which interactions could you make simpler, easier and faster for them? Can you do so to a shocking extent? Could that be a differentiator for your business?

Where do you have a chance to delight your customers? Where could you bring colour, movement, emotion, wonder, joy, humour, personality to their interactions with your business? Can you shock them with small actions that are big in impact? Witness how Zoë Foster Blake's Go-To Skincare business never misses an opportunity to delight with beautiful storytelling and clever copywriting. How could you make the most of every opportunity to be a peacock?

How can you make this everyone's job? And how can you give everyone in your business the tools to succeed? Does your customer service team have the platforms that allow it to make interacting with your business a delight? Does your social media manager have the autonomy to interact delightfully and generously with people online? Do you take every complaint and use it as a chance to put your full selves on display, valuing every single interaction as if it's the most important interaction your business will have this year?

Are you making the most of every touchpoint within your control (AKA owned media) to build brand and 'earn' media (AKA word-of-mouth advocacy) before you worry about how much media you need to buy (AKA advertising)?

Building your business's brand through a commitment to experiences makes the task of brand-building everyone's job. It takes the idea of brand out of the marketing department and into the centre of everything you do. Because your brand doesn't exist—it's just a fancy word for the biases and feelings your customers (and future customers) have towards your business. And every single interaction will shape those biases and feelings.

SEVENTEEN

A people-powered gin family

By the end of 2018, the Four Pillars model had caught fire (in a good way: Cam was always scrupulous about health and safety and making sure those beautiful copper machines never turned into giant bombs). Our focus on winning at home, first at our Distillery, then around the Yarra Valley and Melbourne, then around Australia and then around the world, was paying dividends. The heat and light Cam and his team were creating in Healesville and the strength of feeling our customers and fans (we called them gin friends) had for Four Pillars were driving a level of growth we had never dared dream of just five years earlier.

Despite our growth, we didn't waiver on the model of sharing our gin through hospitality, intimacy, experiences and people, all supported by great storytelling and engagement through our email and social channels.

By the end of 2018, we were exporting to over 20 markets overseas and were available in 21 of the world's top 50 winners of the World's Best Bars awards. Our airport duty-free business was also thriving and, within 12 months, we cracked the top ten gin brands in the world for duty-free sales. Back in Australia, we were fast closing the gap on Hendrick's (we would end up catching them in 2021) and were getting fantastic support from every major booze retailer around the country. In other words, we had every excuse to shift gears and start acting like a big advertising-led brand.

But, instead of acting like a big advertising-led brand, in 2018 we took part in over 300 consumer-facing events, and increased that to over 400 the following year. Four Pillars showed up at an event somewhere in the world every single day for two years!

In addition to that frenetic pace of hand-to-hand combat, playing the game the way only Four Pillars could and certainly in a way that the big global brands couldn't hope to match, we hosted 45 trade groups at our Distillery in 2018 (almost one a week) and were involved in over 60 bar takeovers (turning bars into Four Pillars homes for the night), events, pops-ups and tastings in the trade (more than one a week), all while welcoming 85 000 people to Healesville.

We also ran our first bartender competitions in the UK and Asia, flying the winners (and a few extra people Stu randomly shouted flights to during the UK finals) to Australia to make gin with us.

In other words, the bigger we got, the more we doubled down on our growth theory. This was brand intimacy at scale. And it was scaling! And somewhere among it all, we still found time to celebrate our birthday weekend every December with a fundraiser for community causes that mattered to us. And we continued to make and label small batches of gin for people and causes who mattered to us, from the birth of a bartender's first child to raising money to help pay the legal fees so one of our favourite employees could stay in Australia with her young family (her name's Bina, and the gin was launched at an epic event called Binapalooza, which still brings a tear of joy and pride to my eye).

This was the craft intimacy–led business of our dreams. A business that was showing you could focus everything on making the best possible product you could, and you could commit yourself to a model of growing through smallness: thousands of small acts of storytelling, hospitality, generosity and storydoing. But, as always, with growth comes challenge and change.

The first five years had taken their toll (we were five years older and ten years tired-er), but they had been hugely rewarding (emotionally, if not financially!) and the business was already exceeding our expectations. The question now was whether the business was also exceeding its ability to operate in its current form. Would it need new ways of thinking and working, new ways of growing, new partners to grow with? And, critically, would it need more money to do that? The answers to all these questions would have been challenging enough even if life had otherwise remained completely normal. But in 2020, a new and very challenging normal emerged. How we would navigate that period became the additional and completely unexpected challenge we would have to face down if our tenth birthday was to be as joyous as our fifth.

USEFUL BIT #12:
A FOUR PILLARS EXAMPLE

The examples in this section show how our ways of thinking played out in two ways over the years at Four Pillars. Like our commitment to the craft of making gin, this fundamental philosophy never changed.

First, was absolute clarity on our approach. From the beginning, we talked about being 'makers, not marketers'. We talked about how Four Pillars wasn't a brand, but a business that valued the idea of brand (i.e. the importance of bias and emotion). We talked about how, alongside making gin and making sales, we also were focused on making friends. And we talked about how we believed that biased customers were the most important type of 'advertising' we could have.

What's your business's philosophy on growing your brand and reaching your next customers? For us, it was all about driving word of mouth through great experiences, so no experience was too small for us to focus on.

Second, was absolute clarity on the kinds of experiences that were important to us. In the Useful Bit on page 174, I talked about how we wanted people to feel when seeing or experiencing Four Pillars (that we were the most creative, delicious, well-crafted and fun brand in gin), but this was now about going deeper into how everyone on our team could help deliver a Four Pillars experience, from Naccas (okay, so her real name is Nicole) who has been answering our phones for years to our hospitality, design, social and events teams.

The result was two clear philosophies that underpinned (and continue to underpin) the way we think about how we show up as a business. Like all good (clear and simple) strategic thinking, this should now read as common sense given all I've talked about over the preceding chapters.

OUR EXPERIENCE BELIEF

* WE BELIEVE BIASED
  CUSTOMERS ARE THE BEST
  FORM OF ADVERTISING A
  BRAND CAN HAVE.

OUR COMMUNITY

* WE DON'T HAVE STAFF OR
  CUSTOMERS. WE'RE A GIN
  FAMILY. WE HAVE GIN
  FRIENDS AND GIN LOVERS.

* WE BELIEVE IN
  HOSPITALITY, GENEROSITY
  AND MAKING EVERY
  ENCOUNTER SPECIAL.

* AND NEVER LOSING SIGHT
  OF WHO WE ARE AND
  WHERE WE CAME FROM.

* WE'RE PROVING MODERN
  AUSTRALIA CAN BE THE
  BEST IN THE WORLD... *

Philosophy #1: We're a gin family

The first example gives you a sense of how we've talked about our belief in hospitality, generosity and warmth in every service interaction. We've navigated the good times and the bad by celebrating the wins and apologising for mistakes. We always approach interactions with humanity and treat our whole customer community as part of our gin family.

Philosophy #2: A serious business with not-so-serious creators

The second belief gives you a sense of how we've managed the balancing act at the heart of creating Four Pillars experiences. We always look to strike a balance between the seriousness of our gin craft and the creative energy by not taking ourselves seriously and always giving new friends to Four Pillars the warmest of welcomes.

PART FOUR

Growing

EIGHTEEN

Balancing acts

I have a confession to make. I have a whole cabinet full of business and marketing books, but I've finished hardly any of them. What I usually find valuable is the central idea, something to provoke and shake up my own thinking, and once I've got that idea clear in my mind, I go off and apply it to the things I'm working on and the book gets put back on the shelf, half-finished at best. Not a great track record for someone writing a business book.

One book has stuck with me for years because of the compelling idea captured in its title: *What Got You Here Won't Get You There* by Marshall Goldsmith. The book focuses on leadership habits and behaviours and the need to evolve, grow and adapt as you navigate your career, but the title could just as easily be applied to any business. And as Stu, Cam and I entered our second five years with Four Pillars in 2019, it was a really relevant challenge for us to engage with.

Let's take stock of where we were at the end of 2018, five years into our journey. We had just released our third edition of Australian Christmas Gin, this one featuring a stunning artwork by Melbourne's Stephen Baker. We had also just released our first batch of Sticky Carpet Gin, in honour of the Espy Hotel in St Kilda. And, thanks to our core four gins at the time, we had just sold over half-a-million bottles of gin in a year.

Just four years ago, in 2014, we sold fewer than 20 000 bottles (and even that number was twice our original forecast). Now, four years later, we were 20 times bigger. In five years, Four Pillars was twice the size the entire super-premium gin category had been when we started. In facing this new reality, we had to recognise that some of what had got us this far would continue to propel us forward, but other things would have to evolve. My belief in the intimacy-driven approach to brand-building and marketing had not changed, and Stu and Cam remained utterly committed to engaging our trade partners face to face at every opportunity, but nonetheless things were starting to shift.

Our distribution was growing—we were now becoming a more and more significant player in domestic national retail (like Dan Murphy's and Vintage Cellars); we were starting to see significant growth in airport duty-free (particularly in Melbourne and Sydney airports); and we were exporting to around 25 markets overseas. We were starting to reach 'big brand' scale, but it was critical that we maintained the 'small' DNA that had got us here, albeit while having the humility and curiosity to interrogate which parts of that DNA might not be fit for purpose in the future.

Our growth was being mirrored in other ways too. When we began, we recognised that one of the biggest barriers to our growth was the massive cost of excise and the lack of government support for (or understanding of) the craft distilling industry. Stu recognised that, without a strong collective voice, we'd never be able to effect any real change.

Back in 2014, Stu started to engage the original founders of the Australian Distilling Association (ADA). The ADA had been formed in 2004 and was led for many years by the godfather of Tasmanian whisky distilling, Bill Lark. The association had fallen somewhat dormant and was in need of some new blood on its board, so Stu stepped up and was swiftly elected president. One of Stu's first acts was to suggest reinvigorating the ADA with a conference in late 2014. The timing was perfect. Not only had a new wave of gin distillers arrived on the scene (Melbourne Gin Company had launched just a few weeks before Four

Pillars), but also the Tassie whisky scene was finally starting to get the international recognition it deserved, with Sullivan's Cove being named the world's best whisky at the World Whisky Awards.

The conference in November was held at Starward, another dynamic new player on the Australian craft spirits scene. Stu emceed the day, and I helped run some strategic planning workshops aimed at getting the membership aligned on its purpose. There were fewer than 15 of us in the room that day. Fast-forward to Stu's final conference as ADA president eight years later and there were more than 600 craft Australian distilleries represented in the room, including over 250 gin producers. The growth, thanks in great part to Stu's leadership and Cameron's willingness to mentor and support anyone who came our way, was extraordinary. No wonder both of them have now been inducted into Australian Distilling's Hall of Fame (Stu was the first non-distiller to be inducted).

Back in 2019, we were halfway through this extraordinary period of industry growth, and we were starting to see the impact on the shelves. Four Pillars, Melbourne Gin Company and West Winds had been joined by dozens of new Australian gin brands, and the category was flying. Gin was the fastest growing category in spirits. Super-premium gin was the fastest-growing category within gin. Australian super-premium gin was growing faster than the rest of super-premium. And the fastest-growing super-premium Australian gin, and the brand helping to drive that category growth was, you guessed it, Four Pillars. Growth, however, was both a blessing and a curse. And, to paraphrase old mate Marshall Goldsmith again, the very things that had driven our growth to this point remained critical to our brand but were starting to run out of the steam required to drive our next wave of growth.

The first challenge was a consumer one. The growth of both our brand and our category had been so dramatic that we were now looking to sell Four Pillars to a whole new kind of gin drinker. Our first wave of growth had been driven by people who were already highly engaged gin drinkers and highly curious about craft gin in general and craft Australian gin in particular. Yes, we had a job to do to convert them to our craft Australian gin, but they were ready and willing to have the conversation, to attend a masterclass, to sign up for emails and to buy limited-edition releases. Our next wave of growth would rely on our ability to talk to a much wider consumer group, one that was less engaged around gin and simply looking for something great to purchase, order, drink and gift. How could we reach and talk to this wider audience? And how could we do it in ways that would be engaging to them while not diluting our proposition to our core gin fanbase?

The second challenge was a capacity one. That growth flywheel of innovation, collaboration, hype, release and celebration had served us incredibly well for five years. But the risk was that it was starting to only help us preach to the choir. It was great that we were selling exciting new releases to our existing fans on a regular basis, but what about all the Hendrick's drinkers (and even non-gin drinkers) out there who still hadn't tasted Rare Dry Gin in a perfect G&T with a wedge of orange? Our team still wasn't large, and we could only do so much. Should the focus be on making new gins and making noise around those new gins, or making more of our core signature gins and creating inroads into the wider consumer opportunity with them?

The third challenge was at a category level, and it related specifically to the second-most important product in our portfolio, Bloody Shiraz Gin. The success of Bloody Shiraz was down to many things, not least its delicious drinkability, but not far behind was its absolute scarcity. Bloody Shiraz was (and remains) a vintage product. Our ability to make it is determined and constrained by our ability to secure fruit from that year's Shiraz vintage. The first three releases of Bloody Shiraz each sold out within weeks. The mad rush to grab a bottle or two before it sold out guaranteed the hype and excitement around the following year's release. As we made more each year, always releasing a new vintage at the beginning of June, it started to last a little longer, but it was still selling out well before Christmas.

The category problem was that our trade partners were starting to ask for more and more. And while we were happy with our direct channels, like our mailing lists, selling out fast (leaving us room for the other limited releases in the calendar), we needed those trade channels to help us reach that wider growth consumer (the kind of person who wasn't on our mailing lists).

In particular, one of the growth challenges for Bloody Shiraz was educating people on how to drink it. The early-adopting consumer was fine. They were typically adventurous gin drinkers who liked experimenting at home (and sharing their creations on Facebook and Instagram), but the new-growth consumer who was picking up a bottle at their local bottle shop was more likely to be challenged by exactly how to drink this purple creation that looked and tasted unlike any gin they'd tried before. A huge focus for us was getting Bloody Shiraz Gin listed on bar menus around Australia, both in Bloody G&Ts and in more creative Bloody cocktails (our creative drinks director at the time, James Irvine, called Bloody Shiraz 'bartenders' ketchup' because it had the potential to make any drink taste better).

As we pushed to secure more cocktail menu listings for Bloody Shiraz, we came up against the same challenge we were facing in retail. Bar operators (and particularly the larger bar groups) wanted to know they could rely on having a year-round supply of Bloody Shiraz Gin. How could we have our cake and eat it too? How could we continue to celebrate the unique vintage nature of each year's Bloody Shiraz Gin release (something that implied scarcity and time-limited supply) while also now ensuring year-round supply of Bloody Shiraz Gin for our retail and bar partners?

Our answer was twofold. First, we started to make significantly more Bloody Shiraz Gin, which had great benefits in terms of quality and consistency. The larger volumes allowed Cameron and his team to start filling larger stainless steel tanks for the maceration process, reducing any oxidation of the Shiraz gin, and smoothing out small inconsistencies with different parcels of fruit. Our belief remained that craft was about a commitment to quality and excellence delivered with total consistency, and that craft was an ethos that could scale. Our approach to growing Bloody Shiraz Gin was that ethos at work.

Secondly, to preserve the unique nature of each year's vintage, we started work on an idea to mark and celebrate the 2019 vintage of Bloody Shiraz Gin, giving our direct database (our exclusive Batch No. 1 Club and our wider Wilma's List of gin fans) the chance to buy something one-off and special. For a while, Cameron had been interested in printing directly onto bottles and we decided that the blood-red colour of Bloody Shiraz Gin gave us the perfect canvas to experiment with. We approached the super-talented illustrator Jess Cruickshank to come up with a typographic treatment of Bloody Shiraz Gin that we could print directly onto the glass. The limited-edition bottle was a hit, marking the beginning of a new annual tradition of working with graphic artists to celebrate another vintage of grapey gin blessed by the Shiraz gods.

Two years on we were continuing to wrestle with the same balancing act of doubling down on the annual vintage celebration versus reaching and inspiring even more Australian drinkers to try Bloody Shiraz Gin for the first time. Helping us with the first task was our in-house 'chef' (bearing in mind we still didn't have a kitchen at our Distillery) Matt Wilkinson and our great local mate Nick Gorman from Yarra Valley Caviar.

Matt was tasked with developing new concepts for our Made From Gin offering, and this year he'd come up with the idea of using the Shiraz grape skins left over after pressing the gin in a Bloody Shiraz grape and quince paste, perfect with a cheese plate and a Bloody Sour on a cold winter's night. Meanwhile, Matt and Gormo had got talking and, 25 trials later, the world's first gin-infused salmon caviar was ready to launch, giving us yet more deliciousness to serve up at our Bloody Shiraz launch weekends and celebratory gin dinners.

So that took care of the hype around the vintage release, but what about inspiring the wider drinking public? Those people who still hadn't experienced the life-changing deliciousness of Bloody Shiraz Gin? After all, this was a gin that could inspire even people who didn't usually like gin. And for those gin newbies, it was often a revelation. We built a digital, social and street poster campaign celebrating the idea of having a 'bloody revelation'. Inspired more by fashion content than traditional advertising, we worked with artists to try to visualise the moment when those bloody flavours hit your senses. Unfortunately, I was too close to the concept to notice that it ended up looking like the two models we were using had been shot in the head. Death by Bloody Shiraz was not my intention...

We had tried to grow through leveraging more traditional advertising mediums, while doing it in an artistic way. However, the result was received very differently to our intention, and my confidence in being able to leverage mass advertising in a Four Pillars way was shaken, at least for a while. Nonetheless, the harm to my ego and our confidence as a brand team wasn't reflected out in the world, and both our brand and our Bloody Shiraz continued to grow and grow. But what all this did point to were two other emerging problems: leadership and money.

USEFUL BIT #13:
SIMPLIFYING COMPLEXITY

Okay, so your business is growing. Your category is changing too. And the cultural landscape is shifting, driving changes in the behaviour of your customers. In my experience, having worked with big global brands, with small Aussie start-ups that are now scaling up, with charities, with sporting bodies, with wineries, with arts organisations, and of course, with my own gin business, this growth, this change, can create a huge amount of complexity, paradox and ambiguity.

Instead of being paralysed by it, we need to make sense of it. We need to simplify it. We need to find our way to a plan we can stick to. And it begins with forming a view on:

What's going on?

The aim here is to try to form a view on two (hopefully overlapping) circles of a simple Venn diagram.

- What has driven your growth to date?

- What will drive your growth in the future?

And at the intersection:

- What (internal or external) forces are driving this gap? What underlying changes have they caused. Have those changes found a new steady-state or is that change ongoing? Is there more movement to come?

Get clear on this and the next wave of questions to work through become clear:

- What are the overlaps? Can you invest and double-down there?

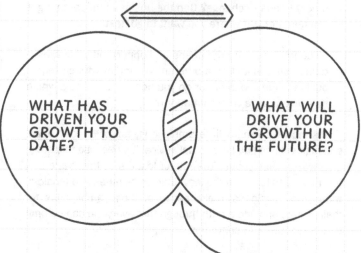

WHAT (INTERNAL OR EXTERNAL) FORCES ARE DRIVING THIS GAP?

WHAT HAS DRIVEN YOUR GROWTH TO DATE?

WHAT WILL DRIVE YOUR GROWTH IN THE FUTURE?

CAN YOU DOUBLE-DOWN ON (AND ENLARGE) THE OVERLAP?

OR

DO YOU NEED TO EMBRACE THE NEW REALITIES OF YOUR NEW OPERATING ENVIRONMENT?

- What can you do to enlarge the overlap? What strategies and plans could feed both sides?

- What are the tensions and choices you're being forced to make? Can you manage them? Can you afford to divide your focus or do you need to make a bold choice?

- What would you need to stop doing in order to be able to commit to the new things you need to do?

- Has the landscape changed so much that your growth theory needs to change? Can the business model that got you here get you where you want to go next?

- If you fully lean into the needs and opportunities of the future, will you just be a different version of your current business (an evolution) or do you need to become a whole new business (a transformation)?

If this model seems a little ambiguous, full of difficult open-ended questions and little actual advice, it's because this stage of growth *is* ambiguous. The role of leaders at this stage in a business is to lean into the inevitable ambiguities and tensions within their business, make sense of those ambiguities for their teams, and find a path through that everyone can commit to and execute with conviction.

There are no easy answers here. Sorry!

NINETEEN

Leading through growth

Our business was growing fast, and by March 2019 we were ready to bring our whole team together for our first-ever all-staff summit at the RACV Club in Healesville. We set out the context for the summit in a few punchy slides. As founders, we emphasised how proud we were of the enormous progress we'd made in just five years, and we balanced that pride with ambition for the next five years.

As we saw it, the first five years had highlighted the opportunity in front of us, thanks in large part to the truly extraordinary family of gins Cameron and his distilling team had developed, and now was the time to double-down on our ambition and our potential. We talked about doing justice to all the accolades the gins were winning, and helping even more people discover and drink better gin. We talked about chasing down Hendrick's and becoming the only major gin market in the world where they weren't number one. And we talked about becoming a truly global brand, albeit one with its roots remaining firmly in Healesville, in the Yarra Valley, in Melbourne, in Victoria and in Australia.

Building on this set-up, we announced that we were launching Four Pillars 2.0. A modern Australian gin-making business based on the same craft-led, intimacy-obsessed values as before, but with an upgraded operating system fit to meet our new realities and new ambitions. At the heart of Four Pillars 2.0 was a commitment to an inspiring (we thought) balancing act: to stay small but *think big*.

Staying small meant doubling-down on our commitment to staying true to what we believed made (and still makes) Four Pillars unique, from the way we make our gin to the way we craft experiences and tell stories. It was about staying focused on quality (above quantity), attention to detail, focus, intimacy and all the million-and-one small things that had made Four Pillars so special from day one. It was a refusal to lose all the impossible-to-replicate things that defined Four Pillars. A refusal to become just another big gin brand.

Thinking big was, in many ways, a more challenging idea. It reminded people that we were defined by quality not size. It asked all our staff to join us in our ambition to do justice to the quality of the gin we were making. And it asked everyone to not fear growth and to embrace the new things we would inevitably have to do in the interests of growing to our full potential.

One of the key elements to thinking big was acknowledging that we would need to professionalise our business and our approach to decisionmaking (without, of course, losing the instinctive magic that had got us this far). There were about 60 people in the room that day, and the majority of the group were working in roles across Healesville (from distilling, bottling and logistics to hospitality, finance and administration). That whole community naturally and happily fell under Cam's remit.

More challenging was the other group who worked in my and Stu's areas. Stu was responsible for relationships and trade, while I was responsible for brand and creative. But, in reality, our efforts were all pointing at the same outcome: growth. And while in the early days, the natural tensions and differences between our focuses were both healthy and easily resolved, now the tensions were bigger, partly because the stakes were higher, partly because we were both placing demands on the same resources (e.g. our staff), and partly because our teams were getting larger and the inevitable differences of opinion and perspective between us were being amplified through our teams.

Over the next couple of years, we experimented with a variety of solutions for this. For a while we tried making Stu responsible for a single weekly 'growth' meeting that pulled everyone together from across our two teams and sought to make sure that our efforts were aligned and our limited resources utilised optimally. Stu, Cam and I tried to stay committed to a weekly co-founders' meeting to maintain the strategic alignment that had always been evident in the early days.

Even then, we didn't always get our calls right, especially with so much happening simultaneously. We had built a brand growth model that was now trying to fire up every part of the Four Pillars machine at once: growing visitation to Healesville; our website direct sales; our retail performance around Australia; our relationships and sales in the Australian bar trade, in over 25 markets overseas, and in airports and duty-free across Asia. And still doing all of it with a small, in-house team of brilliant but stretched people.

There were certainly moments where we moved too fast on small decisions that, fortunately, had no great long-term or negative consequences. An example that always sticks in my mind was when we panicked that excise was pushing the price of our benchmark Navy Strength Gin (that had won more individual golds and trophies than any other gin in our range) out of reach of most people. We took the fast decision to change the size of the bottle to 500 ml so we could keep the price under $100. That decision really pissed some of our fanatics off. Some felt they were being short-changed on the quantity of liquid (they *really* liked their Navy Strength), others felt we were trying to conceal a price rise, and either way, we saw absolutely no sales uplift and ended up going back to a 700 ml bottling. Had we paused to think for a moment, we would have recognised that Navy Strength Gin, bottled in our case at 58.8 per cent alcohol, is a niche product with minimal price elasticity. The products where we needed to be worried about the retail price were Rare Dry Gin and Bloody Shiraz Gin, our core mainstay gins. We really didn't need to waste the effort or cause the angst of fiddling around with a cult classic.

Luckily, the errors we made were all at that level of irritation. They were never really threatening to the vitality of the business, just small annoyances and self-made problems that could perhaps have been avoided had we slowed down for a moment. But that was easier said than done, as we'd spent six years building a business on speed and agility and it wasn't going to slow down now. The biggest learning in hindsight is something that should always have been self-evident to me of all people: communication was key. Whenever Stu and I talked directly, with or without Cam, we would find ourselves in at least 95 per cent agreement, both helping to make the other sharper in their thinking. Sometimes we would have a small disagreement on timing, emphasis or nuance, but we remained as aligned as ever on all the big things.

The challenge was how those small areas of misalignment could get amplified through the Chinese whispers of a growing and geographically dispersed team, all with their own priorities and pressures, and few of whom had learned the balancing acts of our business since day one. Who was I to say that next week's consumer activity was more or less important than the critical quarterly review coming up with the Coles or Dan Murphy's teams? Or that next week's new product photo shoot mattered more or less than the Asian bar conference happening on the same day? In each case, our small business needed to lean on the same resources to support everything, and tensions around prioritisation and focus were inevitable.

There was, of course, one way to ease some of these tensions, and that was to raise more money to grow our team and our business. The need to inject more cash into the business had first arisen in 2015. We were just two years into our journey, and we had blown every financial target out of the water. We were making and selling far more gin than we expected to be doing within three years (which had been the limit of our initial 2013 business plan). We had already purchased and started developing the big timber shed at 2 Lilydale Road, and we'd already ordered our next two stills (Jude and Eileen).

We approached our 20 Ginvestors and asked them if they would like to invest again in the business, this time at a 4x increase on the 2013 valuation. We figured this was fair as round one had seen them invest in an idea, and now that idea had gained some serious traction. We three co-founders were also going to reinvest at that same valuation, and we were going to seek a few new Ginvestors to join the group. All up, 18 of the 20 Ginvestors chose to take up their full allocation at the new valuation, with several increasing their investments above that, and the other two chose to hold onto their initial shareholding. No one sold, and the clamour from new investors to join the party was a huge boost to our belief that we were onto something.

Looking back, one of the best decisions we made was to stick to our guns and our principles through those first two investment rounds. We didn't take on any big, institutional or celebrity investors. We only raised money from patient friends and friends of friends—people who wanted to come along for the journey and trusted us to do the navigating. And, critically, people who expected nothing more than an annual meeting (really a presentation update and a cracking boozy dinner) and a few deliveries of gin releases every year. We couldn't have been luckier with the Ginvestor family we built.

Four years later, in 2019, we were in a very different position. We were starting to reach the limits of the self-funded and Ginvestor-supported model that had got us this far. We had big ambitions to grow our team, our production, our home in Healesville, our investments in duty-free and export markets, and to build a home in Sydney. Plus, we wanted to see our key Australian distribution partner Vanguard grow too, so they could continue to match our ambitions. All signs pointed to finding a bigger, strategic industry partner, someone with the appetite to invest in both Australia's best gin-maker and a specialist premium spirits distributor, and to do so with patience and a priority focus on winning in Australia (while also being able to help fund our growth around the world).

When we laid out the criteria like that, it became clear why, instead of looking to the big global spirits companies (think of famous household names like Diageo, Campari and Bacardi), we instead focused our discussions on an Australian partner, Lion. All of which was why (at that March 2019 all-staff meeting at the RACV Club in Healesville), we returned from lunch to tell our team the news that would be hitting the papers the following day—that Lion would be acquiring a 50 per cent stake in both Four Pillars Gin and Vanguard.

There are many good and insightful books to be written about the challenges of mergers, acquisitions and integrations and what makes the difference between successful and unsuccessful ones. This is not that book, and I'm not the guy to write it. What I will say is that Lion were clearly the right partner for Four Pillars and Vanguard for a number of reasons. First, they placed huge value in the Australian market (they'd been one of the top two brewers in the country for decades and understood the value and potential of the Australian liquor category). Second, they valued and understood hospitality, having built and run vibrant brewery brand homes for the likes of Little Creatures, a true benchmark for hospitality over in Western Australia. Third, they had no pre-existing spirits business, so Four Pillars and Vanguard could help shape the culture of sprits within the Lion business. Fourth, and most importantly, they were good people we could work with.

Led by Managing Director James Brindley, Lion made it clear that they wanted to help grow us, not 'fix' us. James made it clear that he regarded us as the experts in spirits and that he trusted us to continue to run and grow the business our way for the next four years. Lion invested significant cash to support our large capital spending ambitions, most significantly the growth of our Healesville Distillery and the development of our Sydney Laboratory. The plan was for this model and investment to carry us through to 30 June 2023, at which time we would take a fresh look at how we were travelling.

USEFUL BIT #14:
CHOICE MATRICES

Just as all models are wrong (but some are useful), it's also true that almost all models are highly simplistic. There's very little rocket science here, just structures and frameworks to think in. Ultimately, the value you get from a model will be down to the quality of thinking that goes into it. Here's a couple of examples—in the form of two choice matrices. The question they are designed to help you answer is simple:

Of all the things you could do, what will you choose to do?

Decisions are choices. Choices to do things (and not do other things). Your business will not grow because of the quality of your strategy, it will grow because you turn your strategy into action plans that you deliver brilliantly. But your capacity to deliver multiple plans and initiatives brilliantly is limited. You have to make choices—choices about what to do and choices about what not to do.

The idea of a choice matrix is to help you prioritise and focus. I've given you two versions here because different decisions may require different analysis. You can apply both of them, or just one. See how you go. I hope you find this kind of simple thinking as useful for your decision making as I have for mine and my clients over the years.

The ROI matrix

This first matrix simply asks you to consider the return on investment (ROI) you will get from different actions, initiatives and plans. On one axis, cost (you get to define cost, either in pure dollar terms or as a total cost to your business in the form of time, resources, attention, etc.). On the other axis is impact (again, that's for you to define).

I usually draw these up with nine boxes. Plans that fall into box 1 (high cost, low impact) are a no-brainer—there is no ROI here. Plans that fall into box 9 (low cost, high impact) are equally a no-brainer. Everything else becomes a judgement call, but at least now you have a framework to anchor those calls.

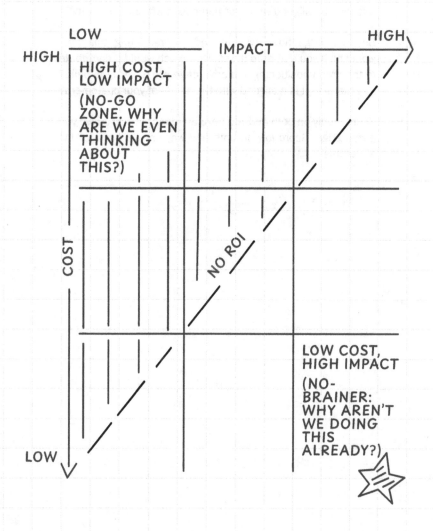

LOW   IMPACT   HIGH

HIGH

HIGH COST,
LOW IMPACT

(NO-GO
ZONE. WHY
ARE WE EVEN
THINKING
ABOUT
THIS?)

COST

NO ROI

LOW COST,
HIGH IMPACT

(NO-
BRAINER:
WHY AREN'T
WE DOING
THIS
ALREADY?)

LOW

The Edge matrix

This second matrix asks you to judge first how achievable the plan or idea is for your business. Does your business have a disproportionate right to execute this well? Would executing this idea be aligned with your purpose, craft and capability?

Second, judge how ownable and differentiating this idea would be if you delivered it well. How much would it contribute to the brand positioning and advantage you're trying to build? To what extent is it aligned with the needs of your customers?

Score highly on both and you have an idea that could give you a real edge. Score low on both and why are we even talking about this?

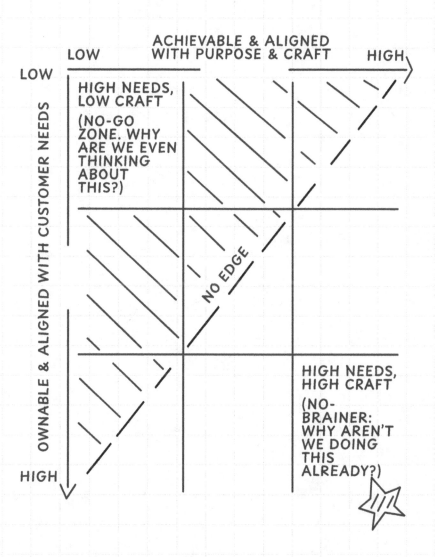

ACHIEVABLE & ALIGNED
WITH PURPOSE & CRAFT

LOW   HIGH

LOW

HIGH NEEDS,
LOW CRAFT

(NO-GO
ZONE. WHY
ARE WE EVEN
THINKING
ABOUT
THIS?)

OWNABLE & ALIGNED WITH CUSTOMER NEEDS

NO EDGE

HIGH NEEDS,
HIGH CRAFT

(NO-
BRAINER:
WHY AREN'T
WE DOING
THIS
ALREADY?)

HIGH

TWENTY

The best in the world...pivoting and staying the course

O n 1 April 2019, Cam, Stu and I woke up for the first time as three full-time employees of Four Pillars. For the first two years, Stu and I had not billed the Four Pillars business for our time, and for the next three years we had only billed two or so days a week, but as much as possible we'd try to keep the cash in the gin business to invest in making more gin, telling more stories, spending more time in the market or buying more production equipment off Cam's seemingly never-ending wish list (we were makers, after all). Now, at last, the business was able to afford to employ all three of us, and we could focus all our time and efforts single-mindedly on Four Pillars.

That focus was much needed because discussions with Lion had been going on since August 2018, which meant that three quarters of the 2018/19 financial year had seen the background machinations of nutting out and finalising the deal with Lion significantly distract both us and James France, owner of our partner Vanguard. Even a good deal with a great partner involves a level of work that goes way beyond the normal, and with running Four Pillars being such a hands-on endeavour, there's no question we took our eye off the ball more than a few times. As a result, we reached the end of the financial year, just three months into our new partnership with Lion, and for the first time since we started in 2013, we hadn't exceeded our growth targets for the year.

Six months later, however, with our focus now firmly back on growing Four Pillars, and with no other distractions, the wind was back in our sails. With the backing of our new partner, we'd been able to secure the long-term lease of a beautiful warehouse space in Sydney's Surry Hills, the future home of the Four Pillars Laboratory, and had begun planning the development of the neighbouring site on Lilydale Road in Healesville, the future home of what we called Healesville 2.0.

We'd also been able to start addressing the limitations of our existing leadership model, bringing in a finance director to balance our co-CEO trio (all of us are, I believe, reasonably business literate, but none of us naturally wore the finance hat when there were more exciting and creative hats to be worn) and a marketing director (who would end up joining us in early 2020). Between those two key hires and the rapid investments Lion started to make in scaling up the Vanguard business, we were well on course to deliver on the 'stay small, think big' mantra we had launched in March 2019.

The gins continued to deliver stellar medal results in top spirits competitions around the world. Between them, our 'big four' gins at the time (Rare Dry Gin, Bloody Shiraz Gin, Navy Strength Gin and Spiced Negroni Gin) won over 20 gold, double gold, masters and trophies (i.e. top gongs) between them. And it was that consistency of excellence that led to the biggest news we'd received since that first overnight email landed from San Francisco back in March 2014.

It was 28 November 2019, and Cameron had flown over to a cold London to attend the International Wine and Spirits Competition annual awards. Four Pillars had been shortlisted for International Gin Producer of the Year, a category we knew a little bit about. The previous two winners had been Hernö from Sweden in 2017 and Kyoto Distillery from Japan in 2018, both distilleries we had collaborated with through our Distiller Series. And now we were up for the trophy.

We won! Just short of our sixth birthday, our little Australian gin distillery had been named the world's best. And this came just days after Four Pillars Gin was the first-ever local distillery to be named Australia's Liquor Brand of the Year at the Australian Liquor Industry Awards. Cam flew back to Australia just in time to join Stu in co-hosting our, by now legendary, Christmas (Gin) Revues in Sydney and Melbourne.

The energy in the room was electric. Here were the co-founders of what was now the world's leading gin producer standing on stage telling stories, making jokes, leading singalongs and serving up a dangerous number of delicious drinks. The artwork on our Christmas Gin that year was a painting of Illawarra flame trees in bloom by Southern Highlands artist Tim Summerton. Stu led a rousing chorus of Cold Chisel's 'Flame Trees' before we ended (as was tradition) with Mariah Carey's 'All I Want For Christmas Is You' with the whole Four Pillars family and half of the attendees all up on stage. For a moment, it felt like all our ambitions were coming true. We really could set a new benchmark for building a craft business (a maker business full of heart, personality and exceptional product) and take it to global scale. What we hadn't counted on was 2020 showing up.

I said in Chapter 19 that this is not a book about mergers and acquisitions, and it's also not a book about Covid (thank goodness). But it's impossible to write about all the decisions, questions, ambiguity and conviction of the next three years without at least touching on the pandemic and the global impacts it had.

The summer of 2019/20 was a horrible one in Australia: a horrendous and deadly bushfire season caused untold damage, hardship and loss of life as the realities of catastrophic climate change really hit home. Rebecca and I were lucky enough to fly away from smoky, smoggy Sydney for a couple of weeks for a family holiday in Vietnam. As we flew home via Hong Kong in late January, we got a sense that something else was up.

Within weeks, it was clear that COVID was going to change our world and our lives, at least for a period. The only questions were how much and how long? Looking back, I'm proud of how early we took the threats of COVID to our business and our people seriously, and got ourselves ready for the decisions that lay ahead. I have no desire to write a blow-by-blow account of what ended up being three COVID-affected years. And no one needs to read my reflections on the experience of trying to work from home while overseeing the education of two primary school–aged kids. So, I just want to focus on four big themes, each of which matters, not just because of COVID, but because of what they revealed and reinforced about the ways we were running Four Pillars.

1. Communication

Communication is key when events are moving fast and facts are evolving in real time. First, there's communication with your partners and fellow leaders, helping you make better decisions together. And then communication with your teams and people on the front line of your business, making sure they understand both the decisions you've made and what those decisions mean for them. I put my cards on the table to Stu and Cam in a very blunt email on 12 March 2020. In it I detailed my views on the very real likelihood of imminent hospitality shut downs (either by us or enforced on us), and how that would affect our staff, our events, our business and our friends in the bar trade.

The following day, our senior leadership team held an urgent meeting to discuss critical points around the business performance for the rest of the financial year (best-, worse-and middle-case scenarios), short-term defensive measures (health and safety, cash flow, staff impacts), implications for the timing and scale of current planned initiatives, and the opportunities that this 'new normal' might bring to mitigate or offset some of the obvious downside risks.

Coming out of this meeting, we quickly sent an email update to our whole business, outlining our responses and how we were going to think about COVID as a business moving forward. We sent the all-staff email on 18 March, just one day after we'd begun demolition works on the old buildings next door. Here was the great irony of our situation: we were just embarking on the biggest and boldest (roughly $7 million!) investment we had ever made, and at the same time, we were sending emails about how we were going to survive until the end of the year. I won't share the whole email here (it was loooooooong) but I do want to share these two extracts because I think they illustrate the clarity and conviction Stu, Cam and I were able to bring to the situation we faced, balancing the short-term response and the long-term ambition.

First, addressing the short-term pressures we could see hitting us fast, we said:

Like many businesses in our industry, the Four Pillars team is a blend of permanent full-time, permanent part-time and casual staff. We are determined to do our best to look after everyone and spread the pain across all our teams, regardless of their employment terms with us.

For our permanent salaried staff, that means there will be cuts to hours and salaries across the whole business effective from 6 April.

We have made the decision for those on lower salaries to take a 10 per cent salary cut and the same reduction in hours, those on higher salaries to take a 15 per cent salary cut and same reduction in hours, and for the three founders to take a 20 per cent salary cut and no reduction in hours.

By doing this, we hope to be able to minimise the impact on our casual staff, and we are asking all our casuals to plan for a likely 10 per cent reduction in their rostered hours.

We want to thank you, each and every one of you, for the support you have shown the business during the past few days as we've delivered this news. We know it's not easy to hear you will be taking home less pay every fortnight, but we think it would be even worse to hear that some of your colleagues would not be coming to work at all next week. We know that without exceptional people, without you, in our business, we are nothing. And we stand together today knowing that we will be stronger as a business and as a collective WHEN, not IF, we get through this.

We will keep you informed if anything changes with salaries and hours but for now we hope these changes will be as far as we need to go until 30 June 2020. At that time, we will undertake a further review of operating revenue and costs and let you know what comes next. Please understand we are all in this together and we want out of this as soon as we can, but we do not think we will be out of the mire much before the end of 2020.

Then, addressing the long-term question of our homes and our ambitions, we said:

Lastly there's the question of our new homes in Sydney and Healesville. It might seem like a strange time to be investing in new hospitality offerings, but after our gin, our craft and our people, there's nothing we believe in more than sharing gin experiences with the world.

So work continues on our Four Pillars Laboratory in Sydney's Surry Hills, with our plan to be open (in a measured and responsible way) in June of this year.

And just yesterday, work began on our new site next door to our current distillery building in Healesville, where we ultimately plan to open an expanded home for both our hospitality and production. It's likely that current events may push back the timing of opening a touch, but the scale of our ambition for our gin, our people and our home town remains undiminished!

A couple of days later we sent a 'Business not as usual' email to every customer on our email database (over 50000 people at that stage). We talked about the four principles that would drive our thinking moving forward. The first two were about supporting the public health system and taking collective responsibility for slowing the spread of the virus. The second two were more specific to our business.

The first of these points was around our staff and our commitment to doing our best to look after everyone who worked at Four Pillars, regardless of their employment terms with us. We undertook to put people first (for example, we immediately suspended all investments in printed collateral and any discretionary costs that we could instead put towards wages), and we committed to spreading the pain evenly and fairly across the whole business. We were determined not to let our casual teams bear the brunt of what was about to happen.

The second point focused on *experiences* and our belief that *experiences matter* and would continue to matter in the post-Covid future. 'Because we have to make sure that the world we navigate towards is one still worth living in' we said, '[a world] where people can share a G&T, and a story and a laugh. One where people can go to a bar or an art gallery or a movie.' We were committed to keeping those connections, and to 'supporting the bars and institutions we love'. We also encouraged our partners across the drinks and hospitality trade to think about how they could 'survive today and thrive again, by serving up hospitality and experiences in new ways.'

The main point of the rest of the email was to explain changes to the operation of our Healesville Distillery door and our masterclasses, but what came back were dozens of emails like this one:

Hey Four Pillars, I love your product, but I REALLY love this COVID-19 response. A beautiful piece of comms and industry leadership - clear, optimistic, realistic and kind.

This was a theme that would continue for the next three years, from both our staff and our customers, and it showed the extent to which we had started to deliver on the fourth pillar of our purpose (to support the community our craft depends on). Our little gin business had become a business that people looked to, trusted and cared about.

2. Pivot with purpose

One thing that started to come up again and again was the question of whether we would make hand sanitiser as a number of distilleries and breweries around the world were doing. At first we were a little sceptical and we didn't want to appear to be making a cash grab out of people's need for hand sanitiser. But then Cameron started to receive calls and emails from people on the front line of our health sector looking for products to use in their hospitals and clinics. He put his thinking cap on.

Cam had already been using the highly alcoholic heads and tails of our distillations (what comes out of our gin stills at the beginning and the end of the process... we only bottle what's called the 'heart') as a cleaning product in the Distillery. He saw that by following the World Health Organization's guidance on turning alcohol into a liquid hand sanitiser, and with the addition of some aloe, he could produce a product at scale. Cleverly, and unlike most distilleries who were shipping small quantities of sanitiser in small plastic bottles, Cameron had the brainwave to ship our product in 1-litre bottles that we could run down the bottling line.

This was a win-win-win. With international air travel pretty much on hold, we had plenty of spare 1-litre glass bottles. By running sanitiser down the bottling line, we created more shifts for our casual and hospitality staff. And what front-line healthcare professionals needed was a high-quality product they could trust, at scale.

While Cam developed the liquid, Rebecca and I worked on the packaging and digital side of things, and the Distillery got ready to bottle and ship it. We ended up making two products. The first, called Take Care and sold at cost, was exclusively for front-line carers. The second, sold at a small margin to help us keep the lights on, was called Heads, Tails and Clean Hands. We only made the consumer product once we were confident the need on the front line had been met. And we only focused on sanitiser production until the global supply chain had caught up. This was a temporary pivot with purpose, and not a new business for us.

On 7 April, we sent an email to 69000 people (our database had grown by over 15000 in a month) announcing that we had pre-sold 20000 bottles of hand sanitiser and were now busy making and shipping it as fast as possible. We finished the email by signing off from every single human in the Four Pillars family, detailing every role they'd been performing before COVID hit and what they were doing now. We wanted to maintain those human connections that had always fuelled our business, and to let people know that their support of Four Pillars translated into support for real people, jobs and families.

3. Staying the course

Alongside this crazy hand sanitiser detour, we also stuck to our core purpose and released a gin we had been working on since Cam, Stu and I took a trip to Japan back in spring 2019. Superficially, we were there to watch my beloved Welsh rugby team play (and beat) the Wallabies at the Rugby World Cup in Tokyo, but there was a deeper business reason too: Cam and Stu had lined up The Kyoto Distillery to be our third Distiller Series partners, and the resulting gin was slated to be released in late March 2020.

After much debate, we decided to stick to our guns and press on with the release of what we called Changing Seasons Gin. The gin was delicious, the label artwork (created by our long-time collaborators Weave in Melbourne) was beautiful, and we figured people could do with some delicious distraction from all the gloom in the world. Changing Seasons Gin went on to be one of our most successful limited-edition releases of all time, giving us confidence that, even if our business wasn't going to be the same for a while (a long while it turned out), it was all going to be okay.

This theme of staying the course continued over the year and years that followed. We pressed on with the development of our expanded Healesville home, we opened our beautiful Laboratory home in Sydney's Surry Hills (including a working still, Eileen, who Cam drove up from Healesville one weekend) and we continued to release countless new gins, from core gins like Olive Leaf Gin and Fresh Yuzu Gin to limited editions like our Rarer series and our collaborations with Stranger and Sons of Goa and Warners in the UK.

4. Culture and community

The last lesson we learned through that challenging COVID period was the value of keeping our team connected and smiling. After experimenting with various forms of digital content, virtual tastings and Instagram live fiascos, we settled on a regular format whenever one of our teams was in lockdown (which, to be honest, usually meant everyone in Victoria).

We called it the Super-Terrific Happy Hour (the best 45 minutes of your week), and Cam and Behn Payten (another Ginvestor, early employee and also co-founder of Payten & Jones, our winemaking mates across the road from the Distillery) would introduce a variety of segments (we would literally commission our staff to write, create and produce content every week) that would have the whole Zoom screen full of Four Pillars people laughing together for an hour at 4 pm on a

Friday afternoon, G&T in hand, and life feeling just a little bit more hopeful again after another long and draining week.

It wasn't all fun though. Our HR team did so much to support people, from allocating time for staff to meet, walk and talk together in small groups, to ensuring that everyone had confidential access to mental health support if they needed it, to sending meals home to people who they knew were doing it tough. But the main thing was that we navigated this unprecedented period more or less unscathed and stronger than ever as a community. Now, we just needed to figure out which parts of our growth plans were still relevant and what needed to be re-thought in the face of a new normal.

The end of 2020, that strangest of years, brought the massive energy boost we all needed, when Four Pillars was named the IWSC International Gin Producer of the Year for the second consecutive year. It was a massive fillip and a tribute to the efforts of our whole business in a crazy year.

We had released so many special gins including a Changing Seasons Gin, Olive Leaf Gin and an Australian Christmas Gin featuring an artwork commissioned from Lucy Dyson, a young Australian artist stuck in Berlin and dreaming of Christmas at home in Australia with friends and family. We had scaled up a hand sanitiser machine from nothing, helped out tens of thousands of Australian healthcare professionals and families, and scaled it back down again within three months. We had opened a drinks-focused cocktail Laboratory in Sydney and built a brilliant drinks and hospitality team there who, thanks to Stu's entrepreneurial leadership, had kept busy batching and selling bottled cocktails whenever we couldn't trade. And we had kept our whole Healesville team busy, employed and (mostly) happy in the face of a hugely trying period.

We knew, however, that not everyone had survived (and thrived in) 2020 as well as we had, so we marked the IWSC win with a letter of thanks to everyone in Victoria. We acknowledged the tough year everyone had experienced and shared our thanks for their support with humility and genuine feeling. It was the most Four Pillars way imaginable to celebrate such a big win, and I ended 2020 with a feeling of huge pride in what we'd built. I had no idea that the next two years would continue to be turned upside down by COVID, or that the end of COVID would simply mark the beginning of years of supply chain and cost-of-living crises. What I did know was that our business would never be the same again, and that whatever future we had been planning for just 18 months earlier when signing the deal with Lion was now going to look very different.

USEFUL BIT #15:
VISUALISING TRANSFORMATION

These Useful Bits have been focused on something more than simply your brand, marketing or communications strategy. What we've been trying to shape here is your growth strategy for your business.

One of the key drivers of success for your growth strategy is to be able to make the end destination clear, tangible, compelling and motivating for all your stakeholders: your co-founders, leaders, investors, partners, and anyone you need to come on the journey with you.

My advice? Write yourself some postcards from the future, and make them as visual and tangible as you can. You may not deliver exactly what you visualise, but the key is to focus on the meaning behind the visualisation and to be able to easily share that inspiring vision with others.

Why is that the right destination or ambition for your business in the future? How can you use a combination of your purpose, your strategy and your ambitions to help guide you through the decisions ahead and remain focused on what's important and what's moving you closer to your goals?

Use whatever tools you have at your disposal to make these postcards from the future as tangible as you can. Storytelling, mood boards, reference images, mock-ups. Vivid description and visualisation is a powerful tool here. It's much easier to rally leaders, staff, investors and partners to a cause or ambition when they can all picture the result in their minds.

The one watch-out is to make sure that, in visualising a transformed future, you're not trying to sell it to yourself and convince yourself of its rightness. After all, we're all prone to falling in love with our own ideas a bit too quickly. Visualise the future on one hand, and keep testing the logic of that future on the other.

WRITE YOURSELF
SOME POSTCARDS
FROM THE
FUTURE

WHAT'S THE
IMAGE ON THE
FRONT OF
EACH?

WHAT'S THE STORY
BEHIND WHAT
(AND WHY) THIS
HAS HAPPENED?

TWENTY-ONE

Questioning everything

Spending 2020 to 2022 becoming experts in navigating a business through the ongoing repercussions of a global pandemic wasn't how Stu, Cam and I had expected to spend the first three years of our partnership with Lion. Aside from learning a lot and deepening our relationships with our customers and staff, the intervention of COVID meant a lot had shifted in our plans.

On the domestic Australia front, the impact on the bar and hospitality sector had been devastating. Fortunately for us, people who were working, living and schooling from home were also drinking well at home, so our retail sales were flying. The result was a business that grew faster than expected, but with a very different shape. Coming out of COVID, we knew the hospitality sector would need to rebuild, and we would need to go on that journey with them.

Internationally, the picture was much bleaker. Our theory of growth in export markets had been the same as our domestic growth theory, but with one exception. In short, we were trying to grow through intimacy, but without the benefits of proximity. What did that mean? We were following the same 'only Four Pillars' approach of winning through hand-to-hand combat, events, experiences, engagement, product innovation, trade partnerships, intimate storytelling, great gin and great fun. This relied on three critical things.

First, we needed the support of the local influential bar trade in each market. Our word-of-mouth model relied on us engaging great bartenders and them becoming the ambassadors for our brand. Seth Godin refers to disproportionately influential spreaders of brands and ideas as 'sneezers'. Literally and figuratively, sneezing was not a viable strategy for growth as COVID shut down hospitality sectors in major cities around the world.

Second, we needed Cam, Stu and our brand ambassadors to be in overseas markets regularly, closing the gap between our Australian home and our overseas partners, friends and drinkers. With global travel frozen, the tyranny of distance bit hard and our reliance on human engagement became a competitive disadvantage.

Third, we needed passionate gin drinkers to discover our brand when travelling through Australia and through international airports across Asia. Again, with international air travel at a standstill, this flywheel of new brand fans quickly stopped working.

In Australia, our craft intimacy model kept working even while our homes and our hospitality partners were closed because we had the strength of our direct-to-consumer engine (the social, email and ecommerce strength we'd been so invested in since our first Pozible campaign) to keep our brand in growth. But, overseas, COVID was the black swan event we couldn't have possibly foreseen that turned our greatest strength (live, uniquely Four Pillars human engagement led by Cam and Stu) into a weakness.

As the world began to properly emerge in 2022, only to be hit by supply chain and cost-of-living crises, we needed to understand the shape and dynamics of our business and where our next wave of growth was going to come from, both domestically and overseas.

Domestically, we were in our ninth year as a business and our brand's growth in Australian retail had already exceeded our ten-year targets. We were ahead of schedule. But that growth also meant that our need to think about who our next customer would be had also become a more urgent conversation than we expected. We had spent eight years driving conversations at a product and new-release level (try our new Bloody Shiraz Gin, Olive Leaf Gin, Fresh Yuzu Gin, limited-edition gin, collab gin, etc. ... you get the picture), now we needed to also communicate a broader idea of Four Pillars. We needed to talk more about what the brand stood for to help us recruit gin drinkers who had never even tried our signature Rare Dry Gin, let alone our more niche releases.

This thought process led us to crystallising what we thought made Four Pillars special, which came down simply to flavour and the unique opportunities of making gin here in Australia. As makers, it made sense for our brand proposition to boil down to our making. We started to plan for our first major advertising campaigns to amplify the simple (and, we believe, true) message that 'nothing tastes like Four Pillars'. Certainly, no one makes gin like Cameron and his Distillery team, and they have the medals, trophies and hall-of-fame certificates to prove it!

Beyond this thinking about our master brand (the unifying idea of Four Pillars, regardless of which of our gins you were talking about), we also started to think deeply about our product, inspired by what we were seeing among ourselves and our core drinkers. Two new product territories came into focus, both of which we would have dismissed instantly in 2013, but both of which seemed to have merit as we started to think about turning ten in 2023.

The first was the whole RTD (ready-to-drink) landscape. Back in 2012, as we started to think about gin, the options for a G&T in a can were very limited (and very unappealing). There was no way Four Pillars would ever go into that game. But a decade later, the landscape had changed. People around Australia (me, Stu and Cam included) wanted to reach for a good G&T instead of a beer or wine, and wanted that option even when we couldn't make a drink from scratch ourselves. The question for Cam became, could we make a *much* better G&T to anything else on the market, and even then, would it deserve the Four Pillars name on the can? Critically, whatever we made would be aimed at our existing drinkers. This was not about chasing a new drinker and damaging or distorting what our brand stood for (craft quality above all), this was about solving a problem we had created: a thirst for a great G&T when out and about at a picnic, a backyard BBQ, the beach, wherever.

Cam took his time, working both on custom gin distillations (making more botanically intense versions of Rare Dry Gin so our cans could taste like a full-strength G&T while meeting the RTD requirements of only being a single standard drink in strength) and on custom tonic recipes, which included a big hit of fresh orange, so the can tasted like a ready-garnished G&T. Finally, after much tasting by Stu and tinkering with the final balancing acts of flavour and sweetness, we had our recipe. My design team came up with a can design that felt boldly Four Pillars and sat perfectly next to the bottled gin, and away we went into RTD land and a world of walk-in fridges and constant price promotions.

Within 18 months, we had a family of four Four Pillars Gin RTDs, two gin and tonics, a gin and soda, and a gin and ginger, each made with a different gin, and each with the potential to introduce one of our signature serves. And not only did we have this new RTD family, but they quickly became the fastest-growing gin RTDs in the country, adding huge new volumes to our business (albeit at *much* lower margins), and adding significant new demands on our production team.

The other new product we developed was in response to the growing trend for drinking less, and often not drinking at all. If the RTDs were perfect for Cam's fishing trips and Stu's love of a game of beach cricket, Four Pillars Bandwagon was perfect for my desire to have something to drink when I wasn't drinking. (As I headed into my late 40s, I was trying to limit my already moderate drinking to a maximum of two or three nights a week.)

We called our non-alcoholic spirits (you can't technically call them gins) Bandwagon because we were literally jumping on the alcohol-free bandwagon that had been started by Seedlip and Lyres, and because we wanted people to be able to 'get on it' even when not drinking. Cameron developed two products, both using our signature Rare Dry Gin botanicals and one adding fresh Shiraz juice. We called them Bandwagon Dry and Bloody Bandwagon, and both took our brand into major supermarket retail for the first time.

As a business that set out to only make gin, we were now making a whole family of gins, plus gin-based bottled cocktails, plus marmalade, salt and chocolate (all Made From Gin), plus a family of RTD canned-gin drinks, plus two alcohol-free botanical spirits. Had we stretched our capabilities and our brand credentials too far or just the right amount? Had we diluted our focus on our core gin business too much? Or had we appropriately broadened the aperture of our business to find more ways to serve our customers in more moments? There are no right answers to these questions. Just decisions, conviction and execution.

What I do know for certain is that, if our domestic business was flying high and simply in need of a willingness to keep asking these kinds of questions, our export business was in a very different state of flux. Coming out of COVID, we saw a dramatic and positive bounce back in our airport duty-free business around Australia and across Asia. But our performance in the now 30+ domestic export markets we were operating in was much more mixed.

A huge amount of change—from changes in personnel on our side to changes in our distribution partners to changes in the hospitality and retail sectors in market—meant that, in many places, it felt like we were back where we were in 2017/18. This mattered because export played two critical roles for our business. First, export success was the ultimate signal of Four Pillars excellence to our domestic market. For Australians travelling overseas to see Four Pillars proudly and beautifully displayed in Singapore's Changi Airport, and being served in great bars in London and New York, and then available in top retail stores overseas, reinforced the sense that what was happening in our Healesville shed was really special and was putting Australian gin where it belonged on the world stage. There's no question in my mind that that export profile helped to drive our domestic growth.

The second role of export markets was, ultimately, to do far more than help drive our domestic growth. It was to overtake our domestic growth. By 2023, more than 70 per cent of Four Pillars sales were still being made somewhere on the Australia continent, meaning that the opportunities for overseas growth were huge. If we were to become the new benchmark for craft gin at a global scale (as we'd agreed in our shared business ambition back in 2013), then we needed to unlock this global opportunity.

To do that, we would need a mindset shift so we could combine the market leadership position we now had in Australia and in airport duty-free (in 2021 we caught up with Hendrick's sales in Australia and we were consistently one of the top-three performers across all gin in Australian travel retail) with a challenger position in our overseas export markets. I'm not sure we were prepared at first to embrace the challenges and ambiguity of this duality. In Australia, we had gotten used to being able to say 'yes' to everything, supporting our direct-to-consumer releases and our collaborative partnerships, while at the same time also supporting our distributed retail business and our long-term retailer partnerships. But in the export space, we needed to be far more particular and forensic with the small, careful bets we could afford to make. Ten years in, we were still learning on the job.

USEFUL BIT #16:
A FOUR PILLARS EXAMPLE

It was in 2018 that we started to get serious about reflecting on what the second five years of Four Pillars could bring.

The first thing we did was restate our commitment to our purpose and our craft-led ethos. We talked a lot about what it would look like to be a craft business at scale, and we translated that into a series of principles that would serve us well (at least until COVID showed up).

The second thing we did was start to visualise what our future state would look like. What did we want to create? Who did we want to partner with? What areas (e.g. sustainability) did we want to invest heavily in?

We divided our thinking into five areas, and while we couldn't have predicted Covid and its massively damaging impacts on hospitality, global travel and the experience economy (and we certainly didn't foresee the global supply chain, and inflation-driven cost-of-living crises that would follow Covid), we did get more of the big bets right than not.

It was thanks to this thinking that we got clear on the need to take on a bigger partner (Lion); that we committed to another property purchase in Healesville to double the size of our Distillery home; and that we developed a second home, a drinks Laboratory in Sydney's Surry Hills. It was also thanks to this thinking that we doubled-down on our commitment to sustainability while also doubling-down on our commitment to creative partnerships (which led to the culture-shaking partnership between Four Pillars Gin and Go-To Skincare).

WHAT'S YOUR PURPOSE?

* ELEVATE THE CRAFT OF DISTILLING GIN

* CELEBRATE THE CRAFT OF THE COCKTAIL

* SHARE THE CRAFT OF MODERN AUSTRALIA

* SUPPORT THE COMMUNITY OUR CRAFT DEPENDS ON

WHAT ARE YOUR PRINCIPLES?

* BE DRIVEN BY OPPORTUNITY AND STRATEGY, NOT BUDGETS.

* KEEP TAKING NEW (EXCITING) RISKS (CRAFT IS ALWAYS PERFECTING, BUT NEVER FINISHED).

* PLAN, ACT, MEASURE, LEARN, ADAPT (STOP, ACCELERATE, PIVOT).

* MAKE OUR SPEED AND AGILITY A COMPETITIVE ADVANTAGE.

* TRUST OUR (STRATEGY AND PURPOSE-DRIVEN) GUTS.

* INVEST (LIMITED) TIME AND RESOURCES WISELY (VALUE THE OPPORTUNITY COST OF EACH DECISION).

WHAT ARE YOUR FIVE BIG BETS?

1. MAKING
2. HOME
3. FRIENDS
4. EXPERIENCES

5. ENGAGEMENT

WHAT WILL IT LOOK LIKE IF YOU SUCCEED?

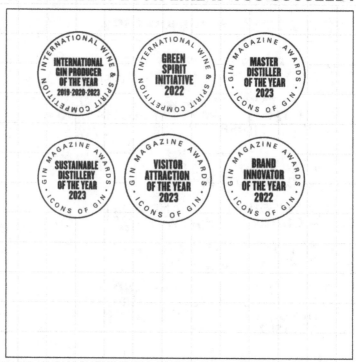

Ultimately, the proof is in the roundels, the awards and accolades we've received in recent years as a result. Awards are not the point, but they are the evidence that something is working. And while our first eight years saw our gins win medal after medal, the awards that have given me the most pleasure in recent years have been for the whole of our business: awards for our Distillery and our production team, for our Distillery visitor experience and our hospitality team, and even for our sustainability efforts and the leadership of our first-ever employee, Michelle Hall, as sustainability leader.

These awards have come about because we figured out early on what we valued, because we kept thinking bigger about what we were really building (beyond just a great product in Rare Dry Gin), and because we had the courage and creativity to keep vocalising and visualising what a bolder future for Four Pillars could look like.

I hope this book, and these Useful Bits in particular, inspire and enable you to think bigger (and also more clearly) about how you can grow whatever it is you want to grow. Cheers to you!

TWENTY-TWO

Ten years down, another decade ahead of us

As much as some things were ambiguous and complex (how to grow an Australian gin brand in the middle of a global cost-of-living crisis and in the face of a newly resurgent tequila and vodka boom was top of that list), other things were absolutely unambiguous. First and foremost, our gin was getting better as our Distillery was getting bigger. Once again, Leah had masterminded a phenomenal development in Healesville, helping us turn the neighbouring site into a brilliant expansion of our Distillery home.

Having lived for so many years with the twin constraints of space and cash, to be developing a vast new site next door, and doing it with significant capital in the bank thanks to our partnership with Lion, was both a luxury and a source of enormous pressure. This was not the time to get lazy with our thinking. Instead, we wanted to be really purposeful with making sure our development dollars created maximum value for our business, our brand and our local community.

The first things to get right were the brief and the partner. The brief we wrote for ourselves was focused on four things (as usual).

1. Future-proof our ability to produce world-class gin at scale

Cam worked with Leah to ensure that we could meet our long-term volume ambitions under one roof while continuing to lift the quality and consistency of the gin we were making. Cam has always believed that our best gins are ahead of us (he still does), so the number one consideration was how to create the space and infrastructure to make more and better gin. Top of that list was a new dedicated space for our bottling line and our bottling crew so we could free up space in the stillhouse for two new large production stills and one new experimental still. All were copper stills made by CARL in Germany, and having run out of founders' mums, we named them Beth, Linda and Coral after the mums of Scott, Elton and Michelle, three of our founding employees. If nothing else, having a still named after your mum is pretty much the ultimate employee retention scheme.

2. Expand capacity to host groups of all different shapes and sizes

Traditionally, we turned bus groups away from our old Distillery door as we didn't want to spoil the tasting experience for regular small groups. But our ambitions were now to lift our annual visitation from around 85 000 people a year to 200 000 people a year, and to be able to do so in all types of weather, from the heat of summer to the cold, wet months of winter. We also wanted to expand our drinks and food options, offering more substantial food offerings and building an experimental drinks capability that matched what was happening up in Sydney (a case of the new Lab teaching the old Distillery dog new tricks).

3. Create a dedicated retail store for our Distillery

Our original distillery door had a stylish corner for retail, which was lovingly merchandised and maintained by Leah, but never enough for our ambitions. After all, a trip to Healesville was only complete if you took a piece of Four Pillars home with you in the form of a bottle of gin and a bunch of inspiration for the drinks you planned to make. We wanted our new distillery home to be a platform to tell our story to visitors through our products and to act as a model of how best to curate our products, showcasing best practice for our retail partners.

4. Starting with sustainability

For the first time, we had the chance to develop a greenfield site from scratch, and Leah and I were determined to choose a partner who shared both our aesthetic and our sustainability values. The partner we chose was Breathe, Melbourne's sustainable architecture icons. The Breathe team worked brilliantly with Leah and our builders to ensure that we took every opportunity to create a better operation and a better experience, while also making sure the whole place was better for the planet too.

Approach the Distillery today and you'll be met by a stunning copper veil. What Cameron thought was just a wanky name for an expensive fence is actually a highly functional design feature. The top half of the veil (just out of reach so no one scalds their hands) is constructed from 1.6 kilometres of narrow copper pipes acting as a heat exchange to passively cool the water from our stills after distillation. The result saves us huge amounts of energy and allows us to return the cooled water to the still system for future distillations, saving gigalitres of water every year too.

Move into the new Beth's Bar and you'll also see an array of copper pipes behind the bar. These are piping gin directly into the bar from the stillhouse, allowing us to save hundreds of kilograms of glass waste every year. All around the place you'll find environmental wins, big and small, with each story told on a black-and-white plaque, ensuring that we do some good for the planet and get the credit for the good that we do. Win-win!

A new era

We opened the doors to Healesville 2.0 in the middle of 2022, just in time for one final year of private ownership before Stu, Cam and I sold our remaining shares to Lion on 1 July 2023. The world remained a challenging place (and I suspect history will show that the challenges we're currently experiencing in 2024 will continue for quite some time), but the business and brand were both in great shape. So why sell? Why not continue to be owners of the business forever?

Every founder will have different reasons for this decision, including, inevitably, the financial one. To found something means to take risk, a lot of risk, with your money (and, likely, home) and oftentimes with other people's money too. At some stage, if you can, that risk deserves some level of reward. Particularly, Stu, Cam and I always felt that the Ginvestors who had backed us unquestionably since the very early days (and with, if we're honest, very little to go on) deserved to have a good day.

Beyond that, we had created something in Four Pillars that was bigger than the three of us. We had built a business with real heart, a business that had a home in the corner of the Yarra Valley, and an army of people who would lie down in traffic (to use a Cameron phrase) to help it succeed. And around that business, we had built a modern classic Australian brand that deserved to stand and grow alongside other modern Australian success stories on both the domestic and world stage, from Aesop and Dinosaur Designs to Koko Black and Go-To Skincare. At some stage, for Four Pillars to achieve its full potential, it couldn't be constrained by the energies and risk appetites of three even balder and older co-founders.

So, the time came to pass on the baton to the Four Pillars team we'd built, the best 150 people we will ever have the privilege of working with. And when it came to celebrating the tenth birthday of Four Pillars in December 2023, we did it in the most Four Pillars way possible. We commissioned the Australian portrait photographer Mia Mala McDonald to capture ten portraits of the people who had defined the first decade of Four Pillars and who embodied the sense of Four Pillars as a gin family.

Some were solo portraits, like our brilliant Marketing Director, Jemma Blanch, also the first (and to this date only) person to ever get married at Four Pillars Distillery. Others were pairs, like Scott and Brett who had started in hospitality together: Scotty running the whole show while Brett moved into distilling and safety at the Distillery, where he still makes sure the world's best gin is made in the safest possible conditions. Or like Elton and Nicole, husband and wife legends of Four Pillars: Nicole on the bottling line; Elton on the tasting bench. And, of course, there were Cam and Wilma, master distiller and the still named after his mum that had started it all.

Stu and I weren't in any of the ten portraits, and rightly so. We weren't the people making the gin, bottling the gin or making the drinks. We were where we belonged, behind the scenes, proudly supporting the best gin-making family in the business, and still telling the stories of the magic that happens in that amazing gin shed in Healesville to anyone who would listen.

A FINAL WORD

As anyone who's worked with me knows, I always say I won't have much to say and then ... well, I talk too much. So it stands to reason that, after so many words, I still have a final word or two to share.

First, as I said at the beginning, this is neither the complete nor the definitive story of Four Pillars Gin. What it is, I hope, is a useful set of highlights that illustrates some of the principles that could be applied to any business or enterprise. If, along the way, I've made you thirsty for a G&T, all the better.

Second, I truly hope that this is a book you come back to often (particularly in the form of some of the Useful Bits). Running a business, growing an organisation, navigating a career...these are all dynamic things, with decisions and choices needing to be made daily. Perhaps in these pages are some models, constructs and ideas that will help you navigate a few of those decisions and choices with clarity.

Last, everything and everyone is different. There are no two same situations, no science, no certainty...just good decisions, good execution and good luck. So focus both on how you can make and execute better decisions *and* focus on what makes you luckier. If there's one thing I've learned from Stu and Cam (and, in reality, there are more things than I can count), it's that being a good human and valuing great relationships with other good humans will always help you be luckier.

So thanks for reading. Good luck. And be lucky.

Cheers friends. Time for one last drink.

DRINKS BREAK NO.4:

Drinking better (gin)

The first three drinks breaks have covered what we once called the ultimate supergroup, the Stevie Wonder, John Lennon and Aretha Franklin of gin drinks. One of the joys of Four Pillars for me over the past ten years has been watching Cameron and his extraordinary distilling team create gin after gin that works deliciously in those core drinks, but also has been able to push the boundaries of where gin drinks go.

This diversity of flavours and possibilities has been leapt upon both by our brilliant in-house drinks teams and by bartenders around Australia and around the world. I am, by no means, the authority on drinks but if you're asking, this final drinks break covers some of my favourites from the past decade.

I've sorted them into four categories: two that are all about flavour, and two that are all about drinking occasions. I hope these drinks inspire you to dig deeper and deeper into the world of great cocktails, drinking better (and not more) as you do it. Cheers!

No.1: Getting festive

From gala dinners to Christmas and New Year's drinks, there's a time for bubbles (of course) and there's a time for cocktails. Here are three of the best cocktails for celebratory moments.

Bloody Spritz

30 ml Bloody Shiraz Gin
90 ml sparkling wine
30 ml ruby red grapefruit juice
30 ml soda water
Grapefruit
Ice

Add Bloody Shiraz Gin, ruby red grapefruit juice and soda water to a wine glass over ice. Top with sparkling wine and garnish with a slice of grapefruit.

Christmas Punch

300 ml Australian Christmas Gin
150 ml Aperol
50 ml Orgeat
300 ml fresh lemon juice
900 ml sparkling wine
200 ml soda water
Festive berries
Orange
Lemon
Ice

Mix Australian Christmas Gin, fresh lemon juice, Aperol and Orgeat in a punch bowl over ice. Top with sparkling wine and soda water. Garnish with festive berries and slices of orange and lemon.

Bramble

45 ml Rare Dry Gin
30 ml fresh lemon juice
10 ml sugar syrup
15 ml crème de mûre
Blackberries
Ice

Shake Rare Dry Gin, fresh lemon juice, sugar syrup and strain into a rocks glass over ice. Cap with crushed ice and float crème de mûre on top. Garnish with a skewer of blackberries.

London Calling

The Bramble was the creation of Dick Bradsell, one of the bartenders who led the charge for the revival of classic cocktails and gin drinks (including another icon, the London Calling). I fell in love with cocktails at bars he created, like Dick's Bar and The Player. And I've served up Brambles at the weddings of two of my closest friends. It's a simple drink to make and one that never fails to delight with its deliciously balanced flavour or vibrant colour.

No.2: Citrus lovers

Four Pillars has been built on our passion for fresh citrus, and there's nothing better than a perfectly made G&T with Rare Dry Gin and a big wedge of orange. However, when you want to take your thirst for citrus to the next level, these are the drinks to do it with.

Southside

45 ml Navy Strength Gin
30 ml lime juice
15 ml sugar syrup
Mint leaves
Ice

Combine Navy Strength Gin, lime juice and sugar syrup in a cocktail shaker with ice. Shake vigorously, and strain into a chilled coupette (curved glass). Garnish with mint leaves.

DIY sugar syrup

You can make your own sugar syrup (also known as simple syrup) at home. Simply cook down equal parts of sugar and water in a saucepan over a medium heat, stirring frequently. Once the sugar has all dissolved set it aside to cool before putting it in a sealed container and keeping it in the fridge. It should last a couple of weeks.

Gimlet

40 ml Navy Strength Gin
20 ml lime cordial
Lime
Ice

One of the all-time classics, use Roses Lime Cordial to be faithful to tradition. Shake Navy Strength Gin and lime cordial with ice in a cocktail shaker, then fine strain into a chilled cocktail glass. Garnish with a lime twist.

Gin Sour

60 ml Spiced Negroni Gin
25 ml fresh lemon juice
15 ml sugar syrup
10 ml Campari
15 ml egg white
Dried orange slice
Ice

Combine Spiced Negroni Gin, fresh lemon juice, sugar syrup, Campari and egg white (one egg should make two gin sours) in a cocktail shaker with ice. Shake well and double strain into a chilled coupette or cocktail glass. Garnish with a dried orange slice.

Bloody Sour

Swap in Bloody Shiraz Gin and lime juice instead of lemon juice and you have yourself a Bloody Sour.

No.3: Bloody drinks

Flavour, flavour, flavour. That's what Four Pillars has always been about, and no gin better encapsulates that flavour obsession than Bloody Shiraz Gin. If you're looking for some fun drinks to make with that bottle of Bloody Shiraz and you want drinks with big, bold flavour, these three will all serve you brilliantly.

Who Shot Tom Collins?

30 ml Rare Dry Gin
15 ml Bloody Shiraz Gin
100 ml old-fashioned lemonade
Lemon
Ice

I love a classic tall, lemony and refreshing Tom Collins. This Bloody Twist on it takes it to the next level and looks stunning in the process. Mix Rare Dry Gin and old-fashioned lemonade in a highball glass and fill with ice. Squeeze in two wedges of lemon and float Bloody Shiraz Gin on top.

Bloody Floradora

50 ml Bloody Shiraz Gin
10 ml raspberry cordial
25 ml lime juice
Ginger beer
Lime
Ice

Squeeze lime juice into a shaker and reserve the lime hulls. Add Bloody Shiraz Gin and raspberry cordial to the shaker, shake vigorously with ice. Strain into a rocks glass and add some ginger beer. Top up with fresh ice and garnish with the lime hull.

New Black

45 ml Bloody Shiraz Gin
20 ml Regal Rogue Wild Rose
2.5 ml Mac. by Brookie's
2.5 ml Mr Black Cold Brew
Ice

Combine Bloody Shiraz Gin, Regal Rogue Wild Rose, Mac. by Brookie's and Mr Black Cold Brew in a mixing glass over a large block of ice.

Aussie coffee culture for the win

You might need to forage on the internet to find some of these ingredients, and don't stress if you need to experiment with alternatives. That's half the fun of drinks-making. In particular, Mr Black is just the tip of the iceberg of a whole wave of great coffee-based spirits coming out of Australia's coffee culture. Try them all!

No.4: Summer drinking

Hot summer evenings call for cool, bright refreshing drinks. These three gin drinks are all made for starting off a summer night in exactly the right place.

Shakey Pete

50 ml fresh lemon juice
50 ml ginger syrup
30 ml Sticky Carpet Gin
6 ice cubes
Pale ale beer
Ice

Put fresh lemon juice, ginger syrup, Sticky Carpet Gin (Rare Dry Gin will work brilliantly too) and 6 ice cubes into a blender. Blend until cubes have dissolved and then pour into frozen beer mug. Top with frothy pale ale and enjoy (but go slow... these are dangerously drinkable and deceptively strong).

Automobile

45 ml Spiced Negroni Gin or Rare Dry Gin
30 ml lime juice
15 ml Grenadine
Ginger beer
Mint
Ice

Add Spiced Negroni Gin or Rare Dry Gin, lime juice and Grenadine to a highball glass over ice. Top with ginger beer and garnish with mint.

Tanlines

This last drink is a cheat as it's not one you could ever hope to make at home. Lucky for you, the Four Pillars Laboratory in Sydney batches and bottles some every week. Move heaven and earth to get a bottle, keep it in the fridge, pour 100ml over ice, garnish with a lime leaf and thank me later.

Summer nostalgia

Gin goes so well with summer, and it was that relationship that inspired James Irvine to invent the ultimate gin-based summer cocktail, Tanlines, when he was developing the first-ever menu for the Four Pillars Laboratory in Sydney. Jimmy wanted to evoke nostalgia for 80s summers of coconut oil and Pina Coladas. Tanlines was the answer and it has never left the Lab menu.

PS: A USEFUL READING LIST

This isn't the kind of book that is full of references and appendices. After all, every model and construct I've shared with you is simply based on something I have picked up or developed along the way and used to help shape the evolution of the Four Pillars business (alongside the unmatched wisdom, instincts, intelligence and talent of Cam and Stu).

I did, however, think it might be useful to share a short follow-up list of things to read and listen to that might help you dig a bit deeper into some of the theories touched on in this book.

I also, like many of you I suspect, spend a great deal of time reading about marketing, brand and business strategy, so I've kept this list very brief. I also value divergent thinking, knowing that inspiration and ideas can come from strange places, so I've included a couple of left-field suggestions too. Happy reading (and thinking).

A weekly habit

The Economist

I've been a subscriber to *The Economist* for as long as I can remember. In a world where news is 24/7 and our social media bubbles are hard to penetrate, *The Economist* offers perspective and breadth. Read this once a week and you'll be 10x more informed.

A couple of useful strategy friends

Mark Pollard & Alex Smith

I don't know if Mark and Alex know each other, but I follow both of them on LinkedIn and subscribe to their newsletters and resources. Both are incredibly generous with the strategic tools and wisdom they share online. If you don't have the resources to bring someone in to help you think strategically you could do far worse than follow these two and draw on the tools they share to help you structure your thinking.

An all-round guru

Seth Godin, This Is Marketing

Seth has written more influential books on marketing and business than I can name. All of them are worth reading, although I particularly enjoy how much of his thinking he was able to bring together in *This Is Marketing*. His podcast, *Akimbo*, is outstanding too.

A brilliant book on thinking

Daniel Pink, A Whole New Mind

I read this book a decade ago, but it only feels more relevant in this brave new world of AI. Daniel Pink is a wonderful storyteller, and he gets you thinking both about the skills you need to develop personally and the skills you need to hire and grow in your team.

My first brand crush

Marty Neumeier, The Brand Gap

Heading into my first interview with a brand agency (Jack Morton) in 2006, I realised my experience and understanding of branding came down to one industry: politics. The book I picked up to help was Marty Neumeier's *The Brand Gap*. According to Marty, brands exist at the intersection of logic and emotion, and 18 years later, my belief in this hasn't changed a bit.

Marketing as behaviour change

Rory Sutherland, Alchemy

I've never met Rory Sutherland, but it strikes me he'd be cracking company at dinner. An ad man to his core, Rory looks at the world through the lens of behavioural science. His book *Alchemy* gets to the heart of why great advertising and great creative work matters so much – not because it wins awards at advertising festivals, but because it changes minds and shapes behaviours for the better. Read this and think about how the simplest things could have a huge impact on the outcomes for your business.

The godfather of 'nudge' theory

Richard Thaler, Nudge

If Rory Sutherland gets your juices flowing, then dig deeper with the godfather of behaviour science, Richard Thaler. His book *Nudge* has had impact way beyond business and marketing, helping to influence the way that public policy is delivered and social impact is pursued. Deep, inspiring stuff.

A tale of success against the odds

Malcolm Gladwell, David and Goliath

You could pick any of Malcolm Gladwell's books and enjoy a rippingly entertaining and brain-stimulating read. For anyone trying to build a small or start-up business, this tale of underdog success and flipping traditional ideas of power and advantage is a great place to start.

Podcasts to inspire your thinking

Diary of a CEO and Acquired

This is hardly an original thought, but I love a podcast. Look out for podcast interviews with authors and thinkers you like: often one 45-minute interview will crystallise their whole thesis and perspective by the time you've finished a train journey or a run. If you're looking for some more regular podcast habits, I think Steven Bartlett gets consistently fascinating guests on to talk about their work and knowledge on his *Diary of a CEO* podcast, and I think the *Acquired* podcast has done an extraordinary job of digging deep (very deep) into some of the greatest business and brand success stories. The key is to open yourself up to irrelevant, divergent ideas and stories...stay broad in your thinking and your inspiration. Don't just keep looking at your own category and competitors.

ACKNOWLEDGEMENTS

I only got to write this book because Four Pillars Gin happened. And Four Pillars wouldn't have happened without a lot of people. Like, a lot lot. From Cam and Stu to Leah, Rebecca and Sally to all our staff (past, present, fulltime and casual) to our Ginvestors. From our distribution partners around the world to all our suppliers and creative partners. From the brilliant folks at Lion who believed in us to the craft spirits powerhouses at Vanguard who helped us grow and grow and grow. From the food and drinks writers who so enthusiastically shared our stories to the industry professionals who sold, served and supported our gins. And, perhaps, above all, from the first 300 people who supported our Pozible campaign back in 2013 to the millions of people who have ordered a Four Pillars drink, bought a bottle and gone on to gift, recommend and rave about our gin to everyone they know. Thank you to every single one of you. Four Pillars is and always will be a gin family, and you're all part of it.

I also only got to write this book because I had learned enough along the way in my pre-gin career to bring something to the gin table. And that also wouldn't have happened without a lot of people. Almost as many people as were on the first list. From my inspiring parents to my brilliant wife, so much learning happens around the dinner table and in the margins of life. From my first civil service line managers who covered my clumsy drafts in red pen to my first mentors in politics. From Tara, Philip and Helen who took a chance on a kid who'd never worked a day in the world of brands or agencies and gave him (i.e. me) a role in a brand agency in 2006 to all the clients, partners and collaborators who made the next decade so exhilarating (special mention to my old crew at Better Happy, my old office mates at Liquid Ideas and my favourite creative humans at Weave).

The truth is that making anything and growing anything is a team sport. I've been lucky (there's the idea of luck and relationships again) to have found myself, time and again surrounded by the best teams and the best people imaginable.

Matt Jones
Co-founder, Four Pillars Gin

INDEX